WRITING IN THE STILL

Anomaly

An anomaly deviates from a norm, is difficult to recognize or classify. *Anomaly* is a series which publishes heterodox, eccentric and heretical works. Mashing fact with fiction, poetry with philosophy, fish with fowl, *Anomaly* is a laboratory of unprecedented writings.

a re.press series

WRITING IN THE STILL

Andrew Benjamin

re.press Melbourne 2023

re.press

http://www.re-press.org

© Andrew Benjamin 2023

The moral rights of the authors have been asserted

This work is 'Open Access', published under a creative commons license which means that you are free to copy, distribute, display, and perform the work as long as you clearly attribute the work to the authors, that you do not use this work for any commercial gain in any form whatsoever and that you in no way alter, transform or build on the work outside of its use in normal academic scholarship without express permission of the author (or their executors) and the publisher of this volume. For any reuse or distribution, you must make clear to others the license terms of this work. For more information see the details of the creative commons licence at this website:
http://creativecommons.org/licenses/by-nc-sa/3.0/

National Library of Australia Cataloguing-in-Publication entry

Cover image: Helen Johnson, The blower, 2015, acrylic on canvas, 34" x 24". Photo: Andrew Curtis.

CONTENTS

The Place of Poetry: Andrew Benjamin's Writing in the Still
by John W Philipps 9

The Angel Stayed 35
Always More.. 41
Facing... 43
Coming Back 45
Timed Light 47
At the moment...................................... 48
Night's Moments 51
Within the Still, Silence.......................... 53
Turning Away 58
Visiting 59
Warmth 68
Holding.. 69
At Dawn.. 70
Bodies Found 71
To have wondered................................... 72
After Hearing Ibn Gabirol.......................... 73
Rembrandt's Homer.................................. 74
Time's Last 75
Looking.. 76
Notes on Poetry 99

ACKNOWLEDGEMENTS

Writings arise by chance and, equally, are the result of the interplay of support and encouragement. Sometimes they stem from having been inspired. For a range of reasons let me thank: Anthony Phelan, Heidrun Freise, Justin Clemens, Paul Ashton, Jane Rendell, Karen MacCormack, Simon Wortham, John Phillips and Howard Caygill.

THE PLACE OF POETRY: ANDREW BENJAMIN'S WRITING IN THE STILL

John W Philipps

1. THE STAY OF ANGELS

> But the sword   320
> Of Michaël from the armoury of God
> Was given him tempered so that neither keen
> Nor solid might resist that edge: it met
> The sword of Satan, with steep force to smite
> Descending, and in half cut sheer; nor stayed,   325
> But, with swift wheel reverse, deep entering, shared
> All his right side.
> (Milton, *Paradise Lost* VI 320-327)

> In that turning, opening the place that wore the auguring,
> bore the warring that attended.
> Though now real: coming there in the conflict.
> One turned against the other.
> (Andrew Benjamin "The Angel Stayed")

"Where was I in all of this?" asks a voice at one point in Andrew Benjamin's "The Angel Stayed," a question that lingers throughout the poems assembled in *Writing in the Still*.

It provokes a further question: to what extent do the poems concern the place where one finds oneself?

This haunting opening poem, which through eight sections situates its reader in the aftermath of a spectral memory, does not immediately suggest a place so much as the allusive echo of a choir of departed angels. The scene—historic in Walter Benjamin's sense of accumulated ruin—gives voice to such questions and recollections, "singing there in the instant," a still voice that patently inhabits discrete moments of silence.[1] The seventh section, "*That Angel should with Angel war*," expands on a baffling instance where Milton's Angel Raphael recalls two armies lined up one against the other. The allusion sees the Angel Michael wielding a sword hewn in God's armoury, using Satan's body as his target, while steeling himself to land a blow that will not need repeating. With a downward stroke he slices Satan's sword in two and in the returning cycle sheers the now fallen Angel almost in half. The reader's incredulous supposition, even before the ethereal substance sutures the evaporating wound, leaving the angel humbled by the memory of pain for the first time, is that this must be poetic spectacle, a staging of epic excess.

> Is this but a place, a role, assigned in the casting?
> Nothing other.

When "The Angel Stayed"—in which a voice as dubious as we are queries the staging of the conflict—still implies that we have witnessed something *real*, we ask: what is this poetry that expects us to treat a scene like that as a depiction of what happened there and as an evocation of what invisibly remains? "The Angel Stayed" assembles evanescent angels. But a single angel, which stays invisibly and lingers silently like a curative presence behind the kinetic scenes of war, might seem to dispute this plurality of what collides in

---

[1]. "The angel would like to stay, awaken the dead, and make whole what has been smashed. But a storm is blowing in from Paradise; it has got caught in his wings with such a violence that the angel can no longer close them." Walter Benjamin, "On the Concept of History," *Selected Writings Vol IV*.

superordinate sets and unsettling inversions. This may not be a multitude so much as a multiple. The angelic counts as one. *Writing in the Still* opens by offering in the place of a classical angelology a question about the angelicity of the angel.

The question focuses on a kind of movement, of turning, which the poems capture in the stay of movement, the stay of turning. What most marks the angel, then, may become evident in poetry, in how it discloses the conflicts that rent apart appearances and in its fixing of voices and scenes that attend for the most part unobserved in the distance of an uncertain intimacy behind the manifest surface of the world. While it is essential in reading not to become too distracted by the allusions—the allusive text admits to an untameable intertextuality beckoning to its implicit confessional content: the angel is always a crowd of angels—the several that are positively signalled shed light on the leverage that these poems take on traditions that today maintain a perplexing currency. "The Angel Stayed" features in principle every angel but showcases them in forms that suture their differences, that is, if the mode of suture takes the form of something perpetually present and irreducibly strange. The pre-Christian angels of Hebraic and Greek descent, the fallen angel, the angel of the lord, the archangels, the *angelus novum*, the angel of history, the necessary angel, the city of angels, the secular angels of modern philosophy: the angelicity of the angel stays in the background behind interminable transformation, division, and betrayal, but as their rule, and as the obscure principle that gives transformation its life. These *prima facie* literary angels appear to the extent that poetry gives them voice.[2] Milton might have offered a

---

2. After Walter Benjamin, Dante maintains as forceful a presence here as Milton, of course, but as will quickly become evident the angels that occupy the stained glass of windows may be as suggestive, and later we will rediscover them in Andrea Mantegna's *Agony*. We should not forget Rembrandt and *The Angel Leaving Tobias and his Family*. Wallace Stevens's "necessary angel" gives voice to Plato's erotic poetry, and in Michel Serres's *Angels: A Modern Myth* (Paris: Flammarion, 1995) they enter the tactile world at *Charles de Gaulle Airport* in Paris at dawn.

viable starting point for the study of angels not only because he constructs his angelology out of an intimidatingly thorough textual archaeology. The angels and their characters, mediated through archives of Jewish and Christian speculation, come largely from The Bible and the Apocrypha yet some appear restricted to early Jewish occult writings while others emanate from Egyptian, neo-Platonic, and Hermetic traditions; among the fallen angels we encounter several ancient pagan deities.[3] But, less diaphanously, the Milton text also teaches its angelology in the voice of Raphael, the poet staging a response to a curious Adam in scenes that approximate the structure of a Christian seminary.[4] The message *is* its medium. Yet the medium betrays its message. The questionable distinction between *discursive* and *intuitive* reason, which his prosody inherits from epic idioms, serves to justify poetic knowledge as unfettered by reason's lessons in understanding and, by the same transgressive rule, more sensitive to the unthinkable. Raphael says to Adam: "discourse is oftenest yours, the latter [intuitive] most is ours, differing but in degree, of kind the same" (V 487-490). The voice we hear in the third section of "The Angel Stayed" ("*non valde bonum*") evokes the querulous student of angelology turning from the angel's teaching and in doing so falling short of what seemed to be on offer in the *becoming-angelic* of the poetic process.

> What would I have been?
> To have been one of them,
> To be counted thus ...

---

3. The topic of Milton's angels maintains a currency in the scholarship. See Raymond Joad, *Milton's Angels: The Early Modern Imagination* (Oxford: Oxford University Press, 2010). Joad's focus on the relation between the literal and the sublimely imaginative taps into centuries of speculation concerning the nature of Milton's poetics. Earlier, William Kolbrener's *Milton's Warring Angels* (Cambridge: Cambridge University Press, 1997) had examined the critical heritage and its conflicts of interpretation concerning the irreconcilable differences between the poetry and the prose and between the satanic and angelic.

4. See James Ross McDonald, "Milton's Tutelary Angels," *SEL Studies in English Literature* 60.1. Winter 2020.

"Time may come," Milton's Raphael seemed to promise, "when men/With angels may participate."[5] In *"non valde bonum"* a question is raised with a disarming fatality, which despite the particularised settings lodges the poems that follow in a kind of *u-topia* that is neither here nor there: "would there have been an opposite ... where a sense of the better might have prevailed?" In place of the scene of warring angels "The Angel Stayed" evokes maxims of movement that stall movement, where the turning of the angel (of angel from angel, of angel returning from its turning) is stilled, leaving nothing better to which one might aspire than this real, but compared to what?[6]

2. OF WRITING IN THE STILL

Andrew Benjamin's latest book after more than thirty-five years of writing arrives uniquely as a collection of poetry. We might therefore approach these poems from a knowledge of Benjamin's distinctive styles as both an indispensable guide and a challenging innovator in fields of contemporary philosophy. Later I will begin to attempt this. But from whatever direction we approach them—as readers of poetry, as literary critics, or as scholars of the philosophy of art—Benjamin's poems confront us each time with the intimacy of an enigma. The enigmatic keeps fascination in play and yet resists every attempt to explain it. The more we focus on the poem the more it diverts our attention until it makes us aware that the enigmatic movements of diversion are the clues to its essence. A complication will arise, for any attempt to place this work within a body of twenty-first century literature, in that the work itself includes within its ensemble of registers reflections on the nature and the place of art and writing. The title *Writing in the Still* signals not only descriptively what will follow beneath but also with subtle force questions the place of writing. And it guides us towards a further question: how does one write about art

---

5. *Paradise Lost* (V 493-494).

6. I hear: "tried to make it real, compared to what?") and Roberta Flack, who sings the classic Eugene Mcdaniels protest song, *Real, Compared to What?*

and writing? The enigma of this poetry confronts its reader with writing's demand. So, we may speculate not only on the place of poetry in a leading body of work that has hitherto adopted more candidly philosophical idioms, but also, with this work as our guide, we may wonder about the place of poetry in the deeper historicity of our time. It will be significant to note that having lived with these poems for some months and in developing the habit of reading them in a single sitting one is made aware of the cyclic quality of *Writing in the Still*. The work is formed in the rhythm of a diversity of genres of prose and verse. The ostensibly briefer lyric forms mingle with longer poems in staged sections. The collection culminates with a substantial piece, "Looking," which adapts what can be written by stretching it out in a novella form. In "Looking" the echoes, remnants, and allusions of the cycle are subtly gathered into the auto-fictional drama we encounter there. The cumulative quality of this selection, and its delicate coherence as a song cycle, establish two related eventualities: first, one reads with the gathering sense that there will have been more; and, second, it remains distinct. *There will have been more*, echoing the future anterior we encounter on several occasions in *Writing in the Still*, evokes the paradox of a synecdoche, according to which the poems open into a world to which they would seem to peculiarly belong and in which uncountable others will have existed. Yet the question of whether or not this world actually exists can never for essential reasons be decided. It is this quality that distinguishes *Writing in the Still* from a philosophy with which it will nonetheless turn out to have had an intimate connection. In the suggestion of a kind of appendix—if indeed such a thing is meaningful here—the collection concludes with a treatise, "Notes on Poetry," that in its formal appearance traces a vanishing line between the literature and the philosophy whose relation I think is likely to serve as the point of departure for any sustained attempt to read the collection.

Never merely impressionistic, these poems discover in writing how to transport their topic by allowing expectation to open into stranger spaces of thought. The second poem in the cycle, "Always More," gently contests the sense of the previous poem's querulous "nothing better," in case that does not already falter in the consistency of its questioning. We are situated "in the now of the sun's first movement." The situation begins by recalling a convention: "oft repeated, charged then as now with/something other." The repetition not only describes the onset of a daily experience, and the sense of the otherness that accompanies it, but also inscribes it inseparably within the numberless events of a literary address to the dawn.[7] If the *dawn song* takes many forms inscribing ceremonial conditions for *expectation*, then it will turn out that under these conditions an expectation gathers that which has silently or invisibly *already* ended, so as to project it towards the future of an action: "The first recalled what had already happened." Conventionally, hope and foreboding oscillate in such moments. But "Always More" breaks down its subtle meditation into the transition described by light emerging from darkness, which is shadowed by the intimation of song—plunging the difference between lighting and sounding into the retreating uncertainty of the moment. The *before dawn* motif in this way provides the occasion for considerations that continue throughout *Writing in the Still*, in which the question is raised of the intersection of sound and sight, and the relation of that intersection to the peculiar dichotomy of darkness and light by which the visual arts build their claim to sense. That is to say, in reading the poems we are situated in the intersections of writing, between visual art and music. The

---

7. In Paradise Lost, the angel Raphael appears like the sun rising over Adam and Eve at dinner time. In two tragic instances the dawn signals the foreboding of an end that is to come but that in principle already has: the burial of Polyneices and its automatic penalty; and the departure into the day of Romeo, whose demise has thus already occurred. As for *Romeo and Juliet*, the play adapts in its five acts the structure of the alba: the song of lovers separating at dawn. Heidegger writes: "Let us think of the sun. Every day it rises and sets for us ... This appearance is historical and it is history [*geschichtlich und Geschichte*], discovered and grounded in poetry and myth [*Sage*] and thus an essential area of our world." *Introduction to Metaphysics* (105).

intersection itself opens up room for speculation where: "There were no moments/other that those awaiting a voice." The still small voice, like the angel singing there in the silence, occurs in the moments of reading that either recall or anticipate; or rather they occur in the obscure division between recollection and anticipation where one should have experienced a presence.

"... a place, a role ...?" The phrase, *the angel stayed*, serves the dual purpose of naming the poem and on an initial supposition describing something an angel did. The passage from naming to narrating insignificantly marks and at the same time transgresses a boundary without which neither the nominal nor the poetic word will have taken shape. The phrase thus exhibits the structure of an irreducible semantic difference. On reflection, it seems not so much to describe as to raise a question concerning the essence of what stays. If the angel offers its name here to that which stays, then in what form is the stay of the angel expressed? The *stay* invites its readers to speculate on what, as it turns out, will have been quite contradictory in the distinctions that form historically around the seemingly inevitable occurrence of semantic difference. What connection pertains between poetry and prose? What takes precedence in the relation between figurative and literal usage? In what qualities lie the differences between the language of discursive and intuitive reason? And what existence is transported by this differing in the word? Readers already familiar with the work of Andrew Benjamin will recognise these questions as amongst those in response to which philosophy proceeds in the playing out of one of its two most enduring motives: the question of the word. We will return to the second of the two motives—that of the time of history—later in this introduction. But already, a question arises about the relation between philosophy and literature that might reasonably affect how readers respond to this collection, in the desire to know more about the intersection between the established works of a leading contemporary philosopher and this new collection representing his poetry.

3. PHILOSOPHY

Writing about poetry occurs in several guises. In this case, the provisional attempt to inform this introduction by situating the poems within an interpretive framework cut from the history of literary reception also depends on a familiarity with Benjamin's philosophy. For many decades he has written extensively in idioms of philosophical argument, the concerns of which turn frequently towards the intersections of philosophy and art, notably literature, painting, sculpture, architecture, photography.[8] In a dubious but customary shorthand the idioms of art come under the rubric of *non-philosophy*, where one can pose the question of the intersection of *philosophy* and *non-philosophy*. A complication emerges in that the categories of *non-philosophy* also contain gestures that operate within philosophy, as ideally controllable elements of philosophical discourse: the figures of rhetoric, of allegory, irony, myth, religion, and other divisions of writing, including (at first peripherally and so with a greater intrusion) choreography, cinematography, cartography, and so on. The point here will emerge in the realization that philosophy becomes what it is in the relations formed between philosophy and non-philosophy. The tension manifested by these intersections exposes the live circuits of a profound historicity in the connection between philosophi-

---

8. The basic writings include two early books: *Translation and the Nature of Philosophy: A New Theory of Words* (London: Routledge, 1989); and *The Plural Event: Descartes, Hegel, Heidegger* (London: Routledge, 1993). *Present Hope: Philosophy, Architecture, Judaism* (London: Routledge 1997) includes an essential reading of the poetry of Celan and Jabes (119-153). Benjamin develops the transformative potential of philosophy's relation to literature in "Philosophy's Other: The Plural Event as 'Literature,'" the key chapter of *Philosophy's Literature* (London: Clinamen, 2001) 71-104. In any engagement with Benjamin's philosophy two recent books have become indispensable: *Towards a Relational Ontology: Philosophy's Other Possibility* (Albany: SUNY, 2015) and *Virtue in Being: Towards an Ethics of the Unconditioned* (Albany: SUNY, 2016). Some short pieces of writing suggest not an alternative to philosophical argument but an adaptation to peculiar demands. Two pieces, "Place" and "On/Within" have a special pertinence here: in *Writing Art and Architecture* (Melbourne: re.press, 2010) 159-167. .

cal and literary expression that remains unresolved, despite the currency of an epoch during which writers sometimes attempt to place the tension itself into suspense; or at least they have allowed themselves to entertain the dream of such a suspension. It is important to raise the question here because in Benjamin's philosophy the tension between *philosophy* and *non-philosophy* performs the work of transformation, which we hear in the phrase *the possibility of philosophy*. The intersection performs. It works to bring about elemental alterations in the sphere of what philosophy can do. What does this mean? It certainly affects what can be written in the introduction to a significant collection of poetry. But more, in the current epoch, the philosophical address touches on the somewhat mystifying conditions that inform escalating and chronically dispiriting events of existence. To this extent, philosophy aims for an ontology, within which one may find grounds for knowledge and understanding, for hope and action, and for rational judgement. Ontology aspires to the role of knowing about the fundaments of existence. It develops as a perpetually novel science of what makes things what they are. The question is formed in the familiar motto: in what lies being *qua* being? The complication, signalled by the deliberate qualification *perpetually novel*, challenges philosophy to an account that is true at once to the consistency of its formulations and to the coherence of its facility for explanation. Yet, the work of philosophy, in so far as this is formed in the adaptive environment of its non-philosophical objects, seems relentlessly challenged by what puts its own consistency and its coherence in peril. What must be acknowledged here, then, is twofold: that the role played by the arts in the transformation of philosophy forms a consistent strand of Benjamin's writing; and that the principle of this intersection is what gives his readings the explanatory force we have learned to anticipate in them. There are no key concepts as such but words and phrases that have remained in play through an eventful publishing schedule and which describe the quality of the conditions that allow philosophy to proceed: anoriginal, plural, differential, eventual, relational. In relation to such descriptors one further grasps a tension between the process of *allowing*, in the simultaneous movement of giving and taking, and the counter-movement of *refusal*. The former allows one to give way enough for a boundary or a frontier to open a little, for things to fray at certain definite edges towards the surprise of the unanticipated alteration.[9] The latter confronts us with a further tension. On one side, certain works of art manifest an "intentional logic" that resists assimilation in staging the interplay between refusal and allowing. On the other side, where philosophy demonstrates a refusal of relationality, especially in the attempt to interpret the relational artwork, the ethical relation is instantiated. So yes, philosophy's other is not merely awaiting the moment when philosophy learns to add it to determinate existence; rather it approximates already the enigma of what remains essentially indeterminable. In relation to this, *allowing* therefore turns up both as part of what philosophy can do and as descriptive of an ethics in action. It allows the other of philosophy to affect an alteration at a vulnerable region. The other of philosophy is not in this sense "allowed" into the interpretive space of a philosophy that had once excluded it. Rather, allowing alters the interpretive framework itself. In the collection, *Philosophy's Literature* (2001), Benjamin most clearly explains while playing out philosophy's essential innovation in the relation to a literature that exposes philosophy to the plural event of its transformation.[10] The "plural event" names the condition that one may be led to suppose underwrites the otherwise untidy circumstances of life. And so, allowing beckons to a condition that might seem all the more obscure for its inescapable presence in everyday existence: in so far as something remains

---

9. See "Notes on Poetry" in *Writing in the Still*.

10. In light of *Writing in the Still*, it is worth rereading the essay, "Philosophy's Other: The Plural Event as Literature," where Benjamin stages the consequences for a philosophy that allows into its rational sphere that which it can never have been predisposed to think: "the incorporation into philosophy of that which had been excluded defines the possibility of philosophical transformation." (98).

what it is, we cannot conceivably both extract it from the relations that constitute it and at the same time allow it to stay intact; yet, given that one cannot separate the thing from the relations that constitute it, it follows that these relations are already what prevent it from staying intact. The attempt automatically places in question the meaning of the thing itself. One must alter the axiom so that we no longer mark *being* by distinguishing individuals from their relations (e.g., their accidents, properties, contingent events, modes of existence, significant others) but recognise instead their intactness as constituted by the principles of relation that also mark its vulnerability. In the world of a relational ontology there simply are no pre-existing individuals. One might begin to borrow the terms of Benjamin's poetics: relationality stays intactness.

In an article from a few years ago celebrating the then recent publication of Benjamin's *Towards a Relational Ontology: Philosophy's Other Possibility* (2015) Dennis J. Schmidt writes, "To read one of Andrew Benjamin's books is to plunge into the deep end of the philosophical pool."[11] His opening statement evokes the situation where an effective evaluation of a particular philosophical work requires a knowledge of the "long-standing and still-ongoing and quite complex philosophical project" in which it serves as an episode.[12] But Schmidt's valuable remarks on specific arguments in the book nevertheless reveal faltering in the field of philosophical debate, in which the question of *agreement* becomes especially troubled. The "few brief remarks" made in the opening pages as a way of outlining the general context for the book under debate serve unintentionally to shift the

---

11. "Between Niobe and Mary: Remarks on Andrew Benjamin's *Towards a Relational Ontology*," *Research in Phenomenology* 47 (2017) 241. These remarks are part of a section based on a panel session, in which Schmidt in this paper and Andrew Cutrofello, in his "*In Media Res*: Andrew Benjamin's Relational Ontology" (229-240), respond to the book. Benjamin writes a brief reply, "Recovering Anoriginal Relationality" (250-261). This is the place to go to find a relational ontology in action. He writes: "What endures in the end is the need for forms of clarification" (250).

12. "Between Niobe and Mary" 241.

stakes of the problem that Benjamin has exposed. Schmidt first raises a question about why, as Benjamin argues, philosophy fails "to sufficiently think the place of relationality in life." [13] He writes, "whether this is constitutive or simply a long-standing tendency and more contingent failing is not always clear, but it is an important question."[14] The question would indeed have been *important* if we were operating with the possibility of philosophy still either correcting its failings or facing up to their inevitability. But the establishment of the *either/or* in its formulation betrays the inability of this line of questioning to grasp relationality as such. With a relational ontology on the horizon one will be led towards a thinking where the constitutive and contingent mutually interfere. If the failure of philosophy to think the place of relationality is constitutive of philosophy then this will be because it is constituted on and inseparable from the contingency of its relations. At this stage of the debate at least twenty-five years of philosophical activity has established this: an obscure principle grounds the possibility of the relational event, which can be designated, if not directly perceived or comprehended. And so, it must be demonstrated. The complication arises that the principle seems to be intrinsically indemonstrable. Here we may recall the fateful words of Aristotle, who writes "for it is uneducated not to know when demonstrations are necessary and when they are not necessary."[15] The reference is to a principle whose event in philosophy massively exceeds Aristotle's introduction to it in *The Metaphysics*, the so-called *law of non-contradiction*. It is not always pertinent—this is certain—but as far as demonstrating it is concerned one needs someone only to deny or to contest it, and so to prove it. And as Aristotle proceeds to show, in his disarming comedy, one needs someone only either to *speak* (by which something is inevitably posited) or to *remain silent* (which reduces the speaker to the status of a still life). It governs the nature of philosophical discourse in general

---

13. "Between Niobe and Mary" 242.
14. "Between Niobe and Mary" 242.
15. *Metaphysics* 1008a.

and propositional logic in particular, where it is imperative that one avoids self-contradiction. Anoriginal relationality seems to me to be similarly unhypothetical. One only needs someone to refuse or in some way to deny or to contain it for its insistence to become evident. Nevertheless, in relation to classical metaphysics, it seems inevitably oriented towards what arrives in Benjamin's philosophy *the other* of logic.

Philosophy's refusal of relationality comes to light in a provisional way when one considers the classical distinction between "poetic colouring" and "plain prose," which Benjamin in his early book on *translation* (1989) analyses in Plato, alongside the initially baffling determination in Heidegger of the Greek *physis* as meaning both "being" and "becoming." The focus of the book (signalled in its subtitle, *A New Theory of Words*) is oriented towards a question concerning the reality that the word inevitably transports. The problem is situated between two epochal names for conflicts that remain radical today. It concerns the nature of words and the relation of the word to what is transported in our use of it. Philosophy, even before we determine *what philosophy is*, seems like it ought to have no trouble addressing the relations—indeed the relativity—that marks existence. But mere relativity is not at stake here, in its play of forces and in the movements of bodies in space and through time; nor is the contentious sense of a relativism in truth and value that some believe characterises the modern or cosmopolitan outlook. Already, in the book on *translation*, Benjamin had identified the qualities of a productive problem that continues to mobilise his writing in philosophy:

> Difference understood as original difference—differential plurality as anoriginal—both emerges in, as well as provides the conditions of possibility for conflicts of interpretation. For philosophical studies this has the fundamentally important consequence of reorienting interpretation, moving it away from concerns with finality and truth and towards the textuality of the object of interpretation.[16]

---

16. Benjamin, *Translation* 38.

A tension arises between two conventional frameworks for understanding language: the word regarded as a lexeme with an arbitrary signified emerging from the differential relations of the system; the word in its nominal capacity evolving and always possibly decaying over time. Benjamin's gambit involves the supposition that the word in its evident unfolding under the possibility of conflicting interpretation transports a situation of irreducible plurality or, as he puts it here, *textuality*. The word *translation* already establishes this in an uncertainty regarding the actual or original meaning of the word *translation* itself. The Greek word *physis* also therefore can mean something like *translation*. The summary I quote here serves in part as a kind of index for these complications, and also as a preliminary statement of the principles that guide Benjamin in his pursuit of the transformation of philosophy. Readers of Benjamin lose out if they cannot grasp the philosophy in both the intricate specificity of its readings and the general implication of the principles that accompany them. We may treat the word *principle* with caution, as it belongs to a philosophical lexicon that has become increasingly doubtful. But as an unhypothetical presupposition it is nevertheless what *allows* philosophy to adapt in response to the enigmatic diversity of its relational objects.

4. POETRY

How does one address an art that, despite coming from as prolific a writer as Benjamin, demands (one feels) a response that exceeds any guidance from received philosophical ideas? If this question is asked from an implicitly scholarly viewpoint, then *Writing in the Still* poses it consistently too, especially in its culminating piece, "Looking." "What, then, to write?" asks the auto-fictional narrator, an art scholar seated in a breakfast room in Tours, while preparing to write on Mantegna's *Christ in the Garden of Olives*. The question encapsulates the lurking provocation that seems to have preceded the accomplishment of writing itself. The concern about how to begin writing has allowed writing. "Looking" is rich in versions of this formula. Like "The Angel Stayed" it is also elaborately allusive. It may be worth noting that the angels stay, not merely in the literal top left corner of Mantegna's painting—the embodiment, perhaps, of the little light and distant warmth the detail of the painting allows and which recollects the before dawn motif of other poems—but also in the enigmatic exchange of looks that arrives as the anecdotal event of a narrative focused persistently on the enigmas of diverted (or distracted) presence, of an intimacy without intimacy, and of how one captures life in the stillness of a static art. The problem as stated is, to begin with, quite a conventional one:

> What he had to get to was a type of writing that moved beyond simple description and which, nonetheless, allowed detail a genuine presence. He has spent years sitting in front of different paintings. If you stay for long enough, he once explained, you can watch them live. If there is an analogy then it is with a naturalist. The life of a painting, perhaps even more so of a sculpture, needs to be observed with as much care and with the endless patience that watching an animal would demand. Life is an activity. Mere description would equate the painting with an already dissected corpse. Neither would be adequate to the presentation of life.

The passage evokes via the naturalist analogy the wider vista and the question of how one captures without halting the vitality of an essentially kinetic reality. The provocation lies in the realization that an art exists, if one attends to it with the patience it demands, where this has already been achieved. By now, one can no longer resist the allusive text. The extremes of which it is capable are effectively demonstrated by Edgar Allan Poe's "The Man of the Crowd," which famously gathers into its narrative the fragments of "a crowd" of texts. If you recall, the narrative voice suggests at first a parody of the naturalist philosopher, as he attempts to fit the individuals and groups seen among the comings and goings of the crowd into descriptive categories, until his reveries break down into confusion when interrupted by a look that defies all attempts to dissect it within his interpretive grid.[17] Benjamin's "Looking," while giving space to a different if equally allusive voice, does adopt the precise anecdotal formula of the prose poem. Here too an unanticipated event provokes questions that turn on the difficult readability of a relation within which a narrator is caught. The intersections of its writing relate poetry to prose and, within prose, fiction transforms naturalist description. "Looking" of course references the visual arts but relates seeing to sculpture, architecture, and especially to the *stillness* of a certain music. It is one of the several poems of the arts that characterise *Writing in the Still*. And it helps bring into focus the semantic exactness of the phrase *in the still*. Writing does not *stay* movement in *the still* so much as movement *stays* in the still.

The simplest way of putting things would be to say something like: *Writing in the Still* arrives as an anthology of poems, a contemporary song cycle with its own force and affect, and thus separated and distinct from the writer's substantial work as a philosopher. If merely this was true it would already be remarkable as an event in the history of the relation between philosophy and poetry.[18] Yet this collection demands of its reader exactly this, that in order to *read*

---

17. The reference to the "The Man of the Crowd" may not be as gratuitous as it appears to be. It has had more luck in literary history in Baudelaire's translation—which somehow in his French becomes more evocative of an incipient poetics—and in becoming the centrepiece of his *Painter of Modern Life*. So later we find it subtly positioned among the texts of Walter Benjamin's *Arcades Project*. The tale itself can serve as something like a relational manifesto.

18. Numerous poets can be said to philosophize in poetry. More seldom do we discover the philosopher poetizing. Maurice Blanchot can be regarded as one of the exceptions. Benjamin's consideration of Blanchot's writing in "Another Naming, A Living Animal: Blanchot's Community," *SubStance* 37, 3, 117 (2008) 207-227, discovers in Blanchot's determination of writing an affinity with a thinking of the animal. A meditation on Goya's dying dog alongside Blanchot's thoughts about the Adamic naming of the animals (by which they are annihilated in their existence) allows Benjamin interestingly to propose the conditions of relationality in terms of a community "in which the animal continues to figure as the site of a continuous negotiation" (225). Again, the continuous presence of a relational demand interrupts any orientation towards finality.

they throw off or at least allow to unravel the yoke of theoretical presupposition. An implicit law demands that we turn to the poetry for an account of it that only poetry can give. Benjamin has provided the means for this in the poetics of the *stay*. And one can track the *stay* of these poems beyond its initial association with the angel.[19] The poem "Warmth" builds a novel syntax around the image of sun on stone. The poem gathers significance in the clarifying echoes of its lines in connection with other moments in the cycle. And again, it foreshadows the play of light in the Mantegna painting. As if in answer to the question, "what, then, to write?" this performs as the commentary: "There was still a playing out/ the moment staying on." A question arises about the lyrical qualities that inform the writing. The *still* goes to work. It vibrates with the *staying* thus rendering *playing out* and *staying on* inherently equivalent in their distance. The redoubling exposes equivalence but excludes any generalising rule. The reference of the poem's title *warmth* comes into view with the appearance of light and stone. The chiasmic coming into view of a feeling: "Seeing the sun on stone/warming seen." An involuntary memory of the "always untouched" angel interferes in the next line: "Remaining untouched/caught in the continuity of a distancing." A warmth that is seen in distance but not felt in proximity might evoke the sense in aesthetics of a kind of sublimity captured in the merest tinge or breath: a touch of the untouchable, a glimpse of a vanishing

---

19. The arrival of the stay in these poems is overdetermined. Initially one thinks that the stay of the angel features as a hypothetical response to Walter Benjamin's "On the Concept of History." But in "The *Stay* of Poetry: Notes on Norma Cole," its sense is worked out in relation to Cole's *Stay Songs for Stanley Whitney*. It allows one to say something about a certain painting that can also be said of a certain poetry concerned with painting: "'Stay' addresses the presence of that which stands forth, taking a stand and being of a certain form. Equally, taken as an imperative, 'stay' means remain and endure (stay here, stay back, stay calm). Staying is remaining. There is therefore an important connection between being, remaining and taking a stand." (reference?). So there's no doubt that the *stay* of poetry signals a philosophical concern with the remaining in presence of a demand. The question of the affinity between the poems of *Writing in the Still* and those of Norma Cole will have to wait for another occasion.

sublime. It is difficult to ignore the famous words of Arthur Schopenhauer: "we see the rays of the setting sun reflected by masses of stone," he had written, "where they illuminate without warming, and are thus favourable to the purest kind of knowledge, not to the will." The example serves the sense of a vanishing warmth recollected in seeing, which challenges knowledge to turn away from willing (from "the principle of life") and so to transition "from the feeling of the beautiful to that of the sublime." The chill of a "warming seen" can perhaps in this way figure as the "touch or breath [*Anhauch*] of the sublime in the beautiful."[20] But the poems of *Writing in the Still* each time hold still: never quite completing the movement of turning away. They fix instead on more intimate structures of experience. The syntax holds the transition in place and in this way transforms its meaning. The effect is to locate transition itself *elsewhere*, so that one does not, in reading these poems, experience a transition from one state to another (an awakening, a realizing, a dawning), but rather the structure of transition itself emerges as constitutive of the state in which one finds oneself. The equivalence constituted between "playing out" and "staying on" approximates the shape of the work itself. It approximates *work* in the sense of what poetry *does*: it goes to work in playing out.

"Warmth" vibrates with the movements recounted in "The Angel Stayed," where:

> The staying stayed the will's
> Withdrawal.

In reading these poems one becomes attuned not to the aesthetics of reading, in which one searches for critical terms adequate to the feelings the work arouses—haunted, inconsolable, curious, dubious—so much as to the topology of their transformations. That is to say, the poems concern the invisible and inaudible hyperspace of relations, the impalpable *real* of feelings and the transformations that betray them. The opening stanza already puts everything in play

---

20. *World as Will and Representation*

and stills play:

> No more, the movement
> The sending and the taking in,
> Countering one with the other.
> Were the angels to return?

To follow the line, one must chart a movement that describes countering it. Neither sending nor taking in, both of which in the wake of the opening gambit of *no more* have already begun by ceasing, but countering "one with the other." Again, one must grasp a movement that stills movement: neither the externalising of a projection nor the internalising of an introjection but a border frozen between any outside or inside and thus holding their difference for a moment in a scene that excludes their separation. What is meant here by moment? A phrase from the poem "Visiting" provides a poetic answer:

> As if from behind a curtain
> a face fleeing in the seeing,
> lingering in its fleeting presence.

The poetic comes to life in the relation of seeing to sounding and in the spacing out of a single moment across the line in the ordinary experience of a glimpse of something evanescent of which, in glimpsing it, one becomes its object. For a moment one sees seeing but only in the spacing out and reversal of the temporal moment. Habits of perception exclude such spacing out from the frame of knowing. In "The Angel Stayed," the return arrives, in a hypothetical form, as a repetition of the anti-kinetic countering. Later, the poem "Coming Back" is dedicated to the movement of the re-turn, but already one can hear in it the turning back of a sending with a taking in. In the question (were they to return?) the angels persist in the self-correcting movement of turning. And with the tentative promise of angels we glimpse the poetic work. It tempts its reader to the curiosity of a kind of dissection. The classical idiom is instantiated in a technique by which certain lexical elements may be recovered and put to work to deform syntactical arrangements that are not commonly suited to the role the work demands of them:

> The staying stayed the will's
> Withdrawal.
> Remembering that there,
> There for the moment, singing.
> Singing there in the instant.

In the singing one hears a movement that would certainly have eluded the expressive resources of poetry had it not been for the existence of habits of usage that give rise to mainstays of conversation that would be unremarkable were it not for the necessity of their potential for the several senses that the poems put to work. A grammatical question is raised in that the stay depends upon the possibilities inherent in the meeting of lexical and syntactical forms: what syntactical arrangements does the position of the stay in the line allow? There exist elements from a common lexicon with often an ancient pedigree that function as if they occupy at once different positions in the phrase. By contrast, it is easier to suppose the phrase *"l'Angel de Dio"* unambiguously determines the angel as singular and as predicated by its being tethered to the lord (there is only one angel, the voice or *breath* of God). The word "stay" succumbs to no such determinacy. We might speculate that it *refuses* it in its staging of the interplay between refusal and transformation. If what the poem does is to *stay* then the *stay* of poetry is what allows the movements the poem stages (the *staying of the stay stayed* ...). The lexicon includes the *stay*, the *still*, and the *hold*. So, a sense of how poetry can work lies in what Benjamin's phrase the "stay of poetry" suggests. But we have heard it too in Ezra Pound's possibly now tiresome but still ambiguous motto: "Literature is news that STAYS news."[21] If the *stay* performs by way of an answer to the question, "what is poetry?" then this will not (despite my dissection) have happened in the explanatory register of criticism so much as in the demonstrations that the poems make in their capacity

---

21. *The ABC* 8

to (be the) answer. So, allowing this answer in the meantime to stay within the sphere of what is questionable, we find ourselves between two registers. The occasion imposes on each a degree of critical uncertainty: the explanatory, sententious discourse of analytic philosophy reaches the edge of its sphere of intelligibility with the possibility for conflicts of interpretation; and the evocative, affective lines of a heterotopic poetry rewrite the laws of intelligibility and thus encroach on the analytic sphere. The stay, which may in our first encounter betray the echo of allusive memories, does not suggest the psychology of an oppressive post-memory so much as the persistence of a situation into which the poem opens.

5. IN THE STILL OF TIME

"Rembrandt's Homer" on a first encounter offers in the modern sense an ecphrastic (or poetic) meditation on a visual artwork.[22] The capacity of writing lies in simultaneously evoking and erasing sense. The irreducibly visual mark of writing that is at the same time audible in the silence of the page, comes into focus. The line steers between the senses and allows a certain thinking to take shape:

> The eyes that could not see
> Open, empty, full though not
> Of what will have been seen
> But shining with the continual
> Promise of what will have been
> Recounted.

What will have been seen in the telling? The arrangement is that of the look that does not see—a feature of a tradition in painting whose focal point is that of blindness. The poem translates Rembrandt's painting sufficiently to capture in it the sense that its *subject* is that of the Homeric epic in the offing, latent in the blindness of painted eyes. The painting serves initially in its evocation as the median

---

22. I am thinking less of Keats and Shelley, the exemplary odes that with gentle insistence refuse their relationality, nor of Berryman's "Winter Landscape," although that inches closer, but more of O'Hara's "Why I am not a Painter," staging a refusal that allows what it refuses.

between two kinds of recounting: between the modern lyric and the classical epic. Even here a quality that consistently marks *Writing in the Still* becomes evident in its singing, in the rhythmic pulse, the pause, the sounding of echoes, and so the thought arises again of the relation between poetry and song.

> Did he sing?
> Would he begin singing?
> Have begun that way?
> Blindness stays sight.
>
> Each voyage, every battle having ended continues.

A mode of questioning takes place in and so gives space to song. In measured stages a counterintuitive temporal pattern emerges in which one need no longer be sure where the poem is in time, because it situates itself in both the before and after of the telling. The second stanza focuses more on the description of visual details: the strange lighting effect of an absence of light and the trade-off between seeing and telling. In the world of "Rembrandt's Homer" the painting becomes a telling, thus eroding the certainty of a difference between seeing and singing. The poem proposes: light in painting depends on its absence and on looking blind. Are we to hear in this the stay of poetry?

The answer lies in a relation that surpasses the play of sensation but which arises nowhere else. Here I must recall the inherent curiosity of the question "Where was I in all of this?" A bottomless depth seems to open up beneath it. To begin with and therefore a bit obscurely this has to do with the relation between the attempt to think *life* and the ethical responsibilities that inevitably emerge in this attempt. Responsibility in this sense belongs to philosophy. It may be staged in literature but, as we have noted, the literary tends also to be marked by its confronting responsibility with the irresponsible. Permit me to veer back towards philosophy for a moment. Benjamin's *Virtue in Being* (2016) unfolds the relationship between ontology and ethics by demonstrating that this relationship has "an already present structuring force within philosophy." In this book Benjamin traces the fateful place of being human for a philosophy that must acknowledge a world "in which," he argues, "the human being is present as an entity within a generalised relational ontology."[23] In their *presence* one ought to be able to capture the relationality of specific kinds of relation. The place of the human in a relational ontology therefore both refuses its assimilation into any anthropocentric grid, in its evident capacity to interrupt interpretive structures, yet also refuses the more popular tendency towards a post-humanism or kinds of trans-humanism in which are dissolved the admittedly fragile continuities of ethical relationships. The question there turns on the "inherently fragile" (finite and contingent) existence of the source of judgements whose presence exceeds the judgments themselves.[24] It concerns a condition that accounts for how ethics is *actualised*. We might acknowledge here that the unhypothetical principle of anoriginal relationality functions exactly as the ethical judgement does, in that by asserting the principle one actualises its continuing force or potentiality. Even before the book on translation we find it at work: "The original as original dis-unity, and not as the simple opposite of unity, will be rethought and rearticulated here in terms of what will henceforth be called *anoriginal heterogeneity*."[25] In this short essay, which significantly derives its demonstrations from readings of painting, Benjamin announces what in the *translation* book is to be regarded as "the passage to philosophy." In this phrase, again a little obscurely to begin with, there

---

23. *Virtue in Being* 1.

24. *Virtue in Being* 168. I cannot here take the time the arguments of this important book demand but it is worth noting that what is entirely distinct in Benjamin's philosophy emerges most forcefully in readings where he brings two crucial philosophical predecessors into contact: Hannah Arendt and Jacques Derrida. What is at stake is a formulation of law that in Derrida follows the structure of "the possible (im)possible," which in Benjamin's argument fails to account for the continuity (here I dare say the *stay*) of ethical relations.

25. "Interpreting Reflections: Painting Mirrors" *OLR* 11 (1989) 37-72.

is to be found a displacement of the concept of time, a concept that in the *translation* book will not be separable from the problem of translation. The heterogeneity of the word transports its *real*, one might say, in what is lost in the exoteric sense of time (there is always too little, it can never be reclaimed, the future gives time in the present for the past). *Writing in the Still* repeatedly interrupts the exoteric experience with the aporia of a temporality in which moments conventionally grasped in terms of *already no longer* or *not yet* stay in the *now*. Perhaps we need a poetry today that confronts us with the extemporal presence of our relationality, not merely in the suspension of temporality but in the vitality of its suspension. The curiosity that marks the poems of *Writing in the Still* betrays an older sense of the word in which the Latin *cura* [care] unfolds into the heterogeneity of caring, curing, troubling, concerning and it meets the *look*, which maintains a presence in the attempt to resist the necropsy evoked in the naturalist dilemma. This curiosity arises in the autopsy—the eye witness that sees itself seeing—the discovery of the human continuing beyond finality.

The Angel Stayed

1.
The Angel Tires

No more, the movement
The sending and the taking in,
Countering one with the other.
Were the angels to return?

The staying stayed the will's
Withdrawal.
Remembering that there,
There for the moment, singing.
Singing there in the instant.

2.
Agonistès

Always in pairing
Another flight felt in the instant.
The pair shone. Fleeing's flight whose
Check failed to hold.
Moments. Neither destructive nor wanting.

A pure moment.
They did not turn
Tearing within an opening, the light continued.

At that moment nothing remained,
Remaining.

3.
Non valde boni

Where was I in all of this?
What would I have been?
To have been one of them,
To be counted thus:

Then, and then.

Would there be an opposite,
Some other way, struggling against this place
And where a sense of the better might have prevailed?

4.
Always descended

And if the angel had been here
What would have been seen?
The question asked—and he turned.
I am quietened.

The butterfly, from flower to flower

Moving unseen. One then another,
From place to place. Were the angels indifferent?
Not a supernal power, no overarching range.
There, there looking—looked at, I stare back—
Not staring just looking
Not seeing, just that. Blank.
Would ... the angels see.

5.

Soundings

And the other cry?
What sound?
Sounding while the angels'
Ground stood—always there, always distancing.
In that opening that seemed to be space,
Seemed empty, there was always one other.
Space. Unnoticed the angels stayed.
Never needing to hold back.
Space charged by a presence unremarked.
I watched waiting, the treetops moved.
Leaves. A whispering, a constancy of sound.
Who spoke?
There the angels remained unheard.
What sounds there were, were always
Something other.
Unvoiced, not voicing, there but
Never beckoning.

6.

Away there

Rather than turning around it, it returned.
Away there. Not two but one.
There yet away. Never to be caught.
There would not be a glance.
Not even fleeting, still, vanishing.
Even if a cheek were touched
Only ever away.
It would not be as though....
And yet, all around there were others.
Having a history, caring, carrying out
Conflicting demands.
Histories overlapping, yet while there, away.

And it had been said.
Ecco l'angel de Dio.
But the others? In the slide away—
Towards? Divisions would only appear
Recounting allowing their appearing.

7.

That Angel should with Angel war

Could this be possible?
Could it have been what took place?
Would angels war?

Is this but a place, a role, assigned in the casting?
Nothing other. As though a presence were misunderstood.
As though that presence had been appropriated
Inappropriately.

Neither warring nor its other. The angels remained.
Watching warring. Never disposed. Never indifferent.
Watching caring. Angels held their place—remaining.

Then there had to be an angel, not there once, but there
In an always that held fast were its mood to change
And the angel turns, turning against
What stood with it.
In that turning, opening the place that wore the auguring ,
bore the warring that attended.
Though now real: coming there in the conflict.
One turned against the other.

8.

Quid accidit?

What happened?
If the question were not asked....
If there had been another way
Of asking, then, then .....

Pausing in this opening, alone
Though, always accompanied,

The always untouched angel
Waiting in a calm that would be
Forever its.
Around the angel. The angel
Stood alone surrounded.
There, there ... an incessant looking
Seeing without notice.
Nothing could have happened.
Though its taking place befalls it.
All in all.

Always More

In the now of the sun's first movement
oft repeated, charged then as now with
something other.
It laid a claim, made claims,
not with demands, nothing demanded.
Worse, it was the light's shine
that insisted.
Tracking back, each move allowed for
a different register
refusing the possibility that every moment was
the last.

At first it was the bird's call,
While heralding others it had been prompted,
having a beginning.
Moments, sounds, all bear within them this other mark.
Bearing was always there.
Unscripted sounds, sounding within. Other moments
registering within. Not just a beginning.
Always more.

Could a figure appear?
From the dark?
In the dark?
To appear: signing.
What sounds would there have been?
To begin? There were no moments
other that those awaiting a voice. A sounding.

Within that moment, awaiting resounds.
Figures formed. Voicing, forming.
In attending there was presence.
Moments began. Light's shade an opening.

Lighting.
The first recalled what had already happened.
Each beginning
another.

Facing

[1]

Would there be another word?

And the eyes looked back,
eyes, and the face's opening.
They held,
holding.
There could be no otherwise.
To escape is to be retained.
A face taining.
Eyes held him.
The stare, his stare, had
lost what force it had.
Looking back was to be looked at.
Control wresting away.

[2]

Door's opening.
On either side containing spaces.

Breath slipped away.
To be regained?
Coming back, breathing again.
Through a window movement
Wind ruffled leaves,

a branch no longer still.
Its displacing barely there.
Through the trees
a face staring.

[3]

Seeing across,
spaces crossed, yet in the crossing
they endured. As though they
hardened, had become a divide holding back
despite the seeing, regardless of the crossing.

And through it all
the slight of movement's distraction.
The holding eye's faltering.
Could a hand have reached out?
Staring was the face's flight from touch.
Staying.
The leaves had darkened.
Those fallen were becoming the ground.
Wintery light, branches hard and frail.

Noticed, unrecognized,
neither giving nor taking
the face's hold remained.
Seeing.
Back.

Coming Back

1.
We heard the day
- a forth, a calling forth.
Had there been what was
announced—was
there in the chance, in
what now appears,
what had been looked for?
Becoming told more.

A slight edge, breaking
through. Would the
call remain?
Stilled echoes.
A word. A word.

2.
In the return, not to time
but to places.
Glimpsing in a now,
created half lit moments. Caught
again, then given over
to another passing.

Moments bordering on recognition.
Sight's invasion. Feeling
demands that the setting alter,

that the place change.
Changing by returning.

3.
Constancy waited.
Not inviting,
yet awaiting allows
no release, no expiation,
tension held out for more.
The movement changed.

That there would be something,
that something would happen,
was understood. The tension,
not dissipated was held
within this understanding.
A door remained shut.
A shutting poised.

Timed Light

Even now,
in the shadows' play.
Cast about with the flicker forth
of lights.

Pauses mattered.
Time was held by light.
Darkening, quickening
then light again.

The play rhymed.
The wind's rhythm held the key.

At the moment

1.

Always - and this has to be the beginning.
Every moment, in the afterwards of a point
from which nothing drifted. As though
noise hung in the air. Time and again
it turned around. The air
being these qualities. Not in the air, as if
it could not rid itself of those other
elements. They were not other. They were
part of it. The air thickened
Cutting through it only deepened what hold
it had. Things change.
Changed in the
absorbing of elements. Transforming in movement's
gradual increase.

2.

And so it appeared. Elements of craft.
Glimpsing - not in the distance
but as this other seeing. The shine held out.
Light caught at the eye. Flickering across, not
loosening its hold but betraying it. Allowing
it to open - allowing in the loosening, in the
dissipation of its hold, that glimpse in which
nothing fled, but another moment
was caught. Not in its fleeing but as the pure mark of a time
that held the edge.
And so it happened. A detail, a moment's presence.

Neither addition nor continuation. Just a glimpse.
The all.
They walked past. And again.

3.
Whispering. A sound not chilled but sudden
in its barely audible interruption. What a light
touch, and yet there. Barely, but with
a force whose intrusive effect was just that.
Augmenting, yet there was no increase.
Weighing in, lighting upon a surface
which, once marked, would bear the touch
as a moment that could not have been excised.
Will a voice begin?
Not the first sound. But sounding in the first beginnings,
a whisper. Just that.
Staying, though no longer a sound. Its effect
becomes the moment of its presence.
Transforming again, whispering.

4.
What would love's mark have been
if it were there for a moment
in a smile's passing hold.
Could such a point stretch or would the all
that will be have been compressed therein?
And in its becoming past, retaining
what had been in a past without end.
The flicker holding as now,
holing attempts to form more.

Here is what there is.
The no more
of the moment that was all.

Night's Moments

1

Wanted to have noted its having happened.
Through a smile - at first an intimation.
a glance
the eyes shine
neither inviting nor resisting.
Resting at moment's edge.

Within your commitments
within the array of your passions each displays, though deeper,
a gentle hear.

What was there at the moment?
A strength
at passion's edge - a smile as a
reminder of gentler possibilities.
For a moment that carries on.

What is held, rocked in a night
that is love's potential, is what happened.
A moment's passing.

2.
Are you there in others' faces?
In a line, a fold, are you present?
Whole in part.

Gestures where you can be seen.
What is seen when you are there?
There is a moment when, in another's face
—a flicker in a face - absence is filled
by a presence resisting location
refusing a name.

Was it only one night?
A resilient endurance
though only in moments.

Within the Still, Silence.

Having seen the silence that was enforced. Its presence writ large. It spoke through the absence of words. An absence that the silence prolonged. It was all the more eloquent because it endured.

Turning, he soon became aware that a presence had been maintained. Continuing through the exertion of a still unnamed power. Ever distancing the voice whose force was withdrawn. Withdrawing continually. While he could see it, noting a presence that harboured, one that could only ever presage, he knew that he had returned. A turning back, the recalled still unsaid.

Was there a trap? He turned between a truth that he knew pertained to him and considerations which, with an apparent ease, could open out. The general always involved the individual. What he sensed however was that independently of this oscillation there was another space. Was there any point in trying to name this space of work? It was not just the personal. As a word it lacked any force. In attempting to locate the right term he felt trapped within an encircling constraint. There was a need for detail. How, if at all, could he move on from his own sense of the truth of silence and thus of its constant link both to loss and to its foundering? The latter giving rise to a specific demand. The limit lay within writing. Not within writing's limits but in the need to differentiate between ways of being present. While his caution was continual what he sensed was the founding hold of intimacy.

A presence, muted, remained. No longer a struggle to acknowledge what was occurring. What endured was a relation between silence and his voicing the concerns of its presence. The silence reached out through the still. The continuity of a touch reverberating within him. It was not as though words had fled to gestures. A flight in which dissipation and vanishing would mark what was happening. There was an addition. It remained. Silence held its place. It was announced without its having to be supplanted.

Silence is not loss. Silence may be the mark of grief however silence cannot be grieved. Silence continues.

If there had been a relation to grief then it was located in the threat of a silence whose communicative force, finally, had lost its connection to the voice. The silence that falters before presence is its having been transformed. A deeper sense of loss would emerge. While silence is the voice that speaks within the absence of sound, silence will have only become possible when that voice can no longer be heard. Perhaps this is why language demands silence. The demand is for a form of insistence. No longer present as a simple assertion, there is a holding back. Holding itself prior to the moment in which the voice coheres within form.

One of his greatest fears is that he would not be able to hear his father's voice. He wrote knowing that this was a voice that no longer had physical presence. As a voice it was silent. Indeed, it only survived now because of that silence. At night, in the still, he could hear its silent presence. If it were to be lost, if, within the still, silent presence no longer had a place, then his father's death would have deepened. It would have acquired another quality. If disappearance is measured then a defining moment is the voice. And yet that voice—the voice that silence allows—can only ever be personal. Remembrance does not necessitate this voice.

How then is its presence to be understood? Moreover, what must be grasped in order that its loss be registered?

Questions, especially in this context, generated little comfort. Nonetheless, they had the acuity of honesty.

He could recall the sound of his father reading. In the synagogue, on Saturday mornings, his father was often called to read the Haftorah. It was the power of his voice. Power had nothing to do with strength; it had to do with quality. The remarkable timbre, its sonorous presence. When his father read in either Hebrew or English, they were voiced. They sounded filling the space. Filling it by becoming it. Closing his eyes he recalled what was now silent. If there is an element that differentiates the intimate then it is that this recalling is not simply remembering. Something, for him, sounds. Remembering seemed to demand a genuine sense of the shared. The silence within intimacy has a more tenuous presence.

Accounting for the tenuous would need to begin with the connection between silence as a prelude and the finality occurring when a voice is lost. Initially it is silence as the moment before. Not a silence that is interrupted but a silence still becoming. A presence that may be voiced. Nonetheless, there will always be an end. The end in question becomes a distancing that cannot be shared. This solitude is not occasioned by death's inevitability but by the more harrowing loss of the voice. With that occurrence a loss will have happened. This enclosing intimacy cannot open. It has been created by a form of separation. The possibility choked him. What it necessitated is a final moment in which there is a sense of loss that that neither resists nor refuses the hold of potentiality. The struggle will be over. There is pure loss. Silence's other. This finality, were a definition necessary, can in part be explained as loss's link to that which has, finally, slipped from recall. All that remains is the impossibility. There is nothing other. The separation of the intimate. Its continual defiance of words.

Here was the difference. Silence allows for its recovery. Silence holds openings, still. Were he to have grieved then it would not be for any absence, if the latter were to have been simply silence. He stopped short. Having reached a point at which the necessary impersonality of writing continued to confront something that writing cannot undertake. Or at least it could not do so intentionally. It was as though a full circle had been turned. He had come back to an engagement with the very form of impossibility with which he had begun.

There couldn't be an aftermath. The struggle was with a form of discontinuity. He had returned. The interruption occurring when the voice is lost, when recall can no longer be staged, is the intimacy of solitude. If there were a limit, one which demands the work of memory, then while there will be a remembering, what cannot be overcome is the opened space of the intimate. The space in which he will fail to recall his father's voice. Even the exercise of force would not have worked. While there was a form of satisfaction since at the limit he had begun to recognise both silence's essential quality as well as the necessity that it be maintained, what was also inescapable was the disclosure of this other possibility. Silence solicites care. Solitude endures untouched.

He could sense differing ways of continuing. If they were to be written the demand would be for a palimpsest. Overlaying possibilities resisting final summation.

Silence is not abstraction. It is another presence, a presence always particularised, and which is there in the moment prior to words, prior even to touch. While there will always that sense of loss and thus the necessity for grief occurring because recall has become impossible, impossibility can become the space of a remembering. Those whose voices will have always been lost, those whose loss continues to defy the intimate, have to be given silence. The giving of silence is an activity. The placing of hope. Turning back, in the turning, he cradled hope silently. Despite this gift, a giving relying on differing forms of anonymity, there is the enclosing. The closing over, thus the maintenance of a space created by recall having become impossible. Not a public impossibility but another that endures. What cannot be overcome and whose work continues is that other disclosure. The spacing which despite an abundance of words can never actually be voiced. Recall's impossibility.

He knew as he wrote that the tear between considerations that allow for hope, and those conveyed by intimacy not only checked the hold of writing, checking it by marking limits, its having been checked meant that solitude persists. What had taken him by surprise was the recognition that writing's limit lay in the disclosed space that cannot be shared. It was this that he had fought to convey.

Turning Away

Turning away.
Whatever prompt there had been,
it no longer mattered.

In the turning...
Not in the after
that would always appear.
Parrying questions.
A slight flicker at the edge.
Was there a space?

It began.
In the turning, a remainder.
Even in the turning, in the opening,
it was memory's work that nagged.
Its film thinly moving
through the space now opening.
What then?

Distancing, the question allowed.
With it, though only there, only
with its vanishing
would there be movement.
A constancy checked, then stilled
for a moment longer.
Still.
Turning.

Visiting

1.
As steps in the past taken,
turned on, and again, the sole sound
as the measure - each step measuring the next.
Would the distance turn, return
and leave just that - the opening
holding all?
Within its measure
a tightening.
What lay in its grip was held in turn,
in the vanishing.

This much,
and with it the question held up
a scattering sound.
Each measure.
Each measures.
Still, the night held.

2.
In the telling
no longer seeking all.
What remained worked against
lament.

Working back
in the turning.
As if from behind a curtain

a face fleeing in the seeing,
lingering in its fleeting presence.
Present, holding,
torn against the time
remaining.

3.
Had often felt the day turn around.
The intrusion.
In the slip holding onto the
now whose escape still beckoned.

Had tried,
in the telling, words upon words.

They flooded in.
The form not broken.
The waves covered - recovered
moments without end - end without end,
words upon words.

With it all, in the sweeping;
form awaiting its gathering.
Form held
holding open, held in the moment.

4.
Passing houses
lit from within.
Two worlds melding in the viewing.

From within an opening enclosed and the intrusion
only noticed as without.
From without glimpsed in the passing.
Confined yet contained.
Locked out by noticing the within.

Connections working with distance.
Particulars in the flow.

5.
Waiting to notice night's hold.
Having slipped its own stay
covering absorbing holding its own.

Slipping free,
Announcing the having already entered.
Already there in the proclamation
turning silence, since silence
hovered in the all.

And in the beginning there
would have been more?

6.
Description offered little
as though the addition of words
carved deeper
displayed more.
Night's word fell away.
Holding out - holding on,

in the turning, to the place opening
beneath.

What little more there was
would not be lost.

7.
And it started,
though perhaps it had always been
and the stark
stare - of its opening - always
and the fell of it.

Once again, in the sweep
swept past and away, and the night's
breaking - broke holding
in the opening, returning
and the ending continued.

8.
Against the curb
the road ran hard,
forcing feet to lift.
At that moment,
the moment of meeting, the
road had given way.

The curb barely touched -
the dust had gathered held
tight by an opening yielding.

At a point - not touching.
At a point - a crack
the opening out.

Dust, dirt and the traces of passing
had gathered.
Locked, held,
within the fragility of place.
Of the passing night,
the wind moving - the trapped
now turning - in its passing - other traces
will, for awhile
be held, captured,
in a place always yielding.

9.
Children played
in their differences.
Playing with it
size, weight, mattered - though in the play.
Play, movement, resisting commitment's eventual withering,
Children played in the sing song,
in the now of accord.
Its possibility at work in play itself.

10.
Languages worked against each other.
Not at war, but overlapping without connection.
And the wind in the trees

the cicadas' almost endless pleading,
the birds sounding.
They neither interfered nor completed.
They strengthened the depth of sound
Playing itself out.

It was language that survived.
What play there was will end.
Connections - present, absent - demand.
They were there in the overlapping.
Birds remained in flight.

II.
The heat held the day.
Village paths led away
from the hill.
The path trod lay beneath
its slow circling leading away.

The day played out
played in the heat.
The butterfly moved flitting,
place after place.
Its speed not matched by the day's
slow drift.
Between them
the day's measure and the butterfly's rapid
back and forth,
was another pace.
Each step measured the way.

Another coming and going.
A different measure
measuring the hold,
the coming forth.

12.
A pigeon picking at what
remained.
Bread torn from a loaf.
Neither cast nor left.
On the road by the gutter
it marked a place.
Passed though not passed.
There as the pigeon, now another,
edged forward and back
completing with a rapidity
that measured the place.

Could there have been another?
A different measure - rather than
what remains - still -
indifferent to any observation.

The bread is not vanishing.
It will, at a certain moment
cease to mark a place.

13.
Water on the streets drying.
Last night's rain fading

slowly.
In the vanishing.
In the fading.
There could not have been a moment.
Only the work,
only the movement.
Fading.

And yet no sign
nothing can be seen except
the movement's traces.
The slow emerging marks,
marking, always afterwards, the passing.

14.
What had altered?
What counted as an answer
impinges, having felt the loss.
As if there had been
another way.

Turning to see in the absence
a face vanishing yet staring back.
Perhaps, the haunt of memory.
The vanishing remaining,

A face appeared
staring back
with its disappearing
a voice not voiced remains.

15.
Marking the changes
drawn to places where the heightening held.
Each based its turn in a sequence bidden.

And,
to bid, to open up the place -
allowing a returning
indifference refused
as necessity insisted.

And if there had been a choice?
Each step already taken
its turn marked a return
within memory's holding forth.

Warmth

There was still a playing out.
The moment staying on.

Lights continued.
Stones warmed.
Shadows past.

Were there others?
And to answer....?

Halting.
Haltering.

Seeing the sun on stone.
Warming seen.

Remaining untouched
caught in the continuity of a distancing.
Seeing within separation.

Holding

What of the holding?
The hand that reached across
taking the moment. Fingers slipped through
grasping.

What held back?
Knowing lasted, though the moments
began to lapse.
Faltering , though in stepping aside
there was another.
Sending, opening:
Awaiting there,
touching, almost.

Still, the hand held.
Would it wait?

At Dawn

What now? The light edged its way
across the sky now yielding its dark.
Waiting there. Awaiting the slight mark,
the filling light as the alterations processed.
No holding back. Today, now, restraint's release.
Moments changing.
Shades, then the light's lines.
Light had found its mark within the day's opening.

The day now holding. Traces having vanished
or rather transferred.
Incorporated. There as memories.
Dissipating within. A suffused force.
A spread.
Allowing the eye to see.

Bodies Found

Arrayed as if the night had
carried them. Though left,
perhaps abandoned at the edge.
The light had gone. If feeling
had been possible they would have cowered.
Huddled closer hoping for an impossible warmth.
They were simply cast.
Devoid of breath's possibility, they remained.

Now strangers to each other.
The body's history is decay.
It can know no choice.
Though the body opens, it calls
beyond its own unmaking.
Remembering allows.

To have wondered

Still wondered what was held open. As though a question whose force had been held back now exerted a hold. Each command called the others. It was not as though he was deaf. Indifference seemed the only word that would have been able to describe what had happened. It was later in the afternoon. Initially the wind comforted him. More a breeze than anything more severe. His body responded. His cheeks were now cold. It allowed him to feel the sun's warmth. Its capacity to warm seemed to work its way through what would otherwise have been mere cold. The interplay of the sun and the breeze, this odd mixture, one allowing the effect of the other to be registered, meant that he felt. Whatever time there had been it was over. There was little point waiting. He was caught in what remained, in the space that had opened. He would try again. Thinking through what had just taken place, he had been afforded neither answer nor chance to move on. If a trap held, such that any movement would cause pain, then he wasn't trapped. It was as though something else had taken place.

After Hearing Ibn Gabirol

I cannot rejoice. My soul is undone.
Were it to change, were there to be another,
Then, and now time's own moving moves me on.
In changing, I can.

There, though without it having a name.
Pressing upon me, a force robbing me of one.
Robbed, running towards what distances me
In the opening, struggling to name, there is another force.

The limit betrayed. If there is sorrow, it does not end there.
Living with sorrow, in it, in becoming myself, returning
And discovering what I may be, holding on to the power
Making me, allowing me, then, only then, is there another joy.

Rembrandt's Homer

The eyes that could not see
Open, empty, full though not
Of what will have been seen
But shining with the continual
Promise of what will have been
Recounted.
Did he sing?
Would he begin singing?
Have begun that way?
Blindness stays sight.
Each voyage, every battle having ended continues.

Cap, shawl, beard
Each—their own way.
Hands clear, yet the painted sleeves
Allow the slightest blur.
The shawl's gold, face and nose
Lit. Though from above? Illumined.
Light would have remained unseen,
Unnecessary and unseen.
The moving hands gesture, what is there
Is not just there in the seeing.
An accord. The gesture here: gesture to what?
Gesturing to the stopped eye, opening,
Opening and continuing in the telling.

Time's Last

Would this be that last time? As though time gave itself, determined forever in a promise not just to be the same but to be curtailed. As if it could be known, knowing that this moment, this instant would be a curtailing. There would only ever have been that time, the time in which it was brought to an end. Seen from afar. Never close. Closeness's own impossibility was the vanishing.

Was there another hope? Hoped for. Hoping for? Was that time's extension? Not time's, rather the time that would have been, that last time.

It was not as though all that remained were unimportant remnants. Something was there. Elusive, only there to be discerned, a lighting force.

Looking

1) Looking, Writing

What would it mean to lay a claim to writing? A claim to be made after what is now decades of work. This was the reflection. Hardly singular, though that was the initial formulation. Even allowing the question to be asked has to be understood as more than mere questioning. Where was he with it? What seemed to matter was not a definition of himself in relation to writing. The latter would always be more than an act of production. And yet such a concession could be scarcely admitted. The question took him elsewhere. Writing, for this is what he did, directed him. The question that he continued to ask concerned what was there, there continually pushing at the limits that were encountered. Their imposition beckoned.

What would have made him write it?

That the question could even be admitted and that it might be considered worthy of response seemed a presumption not even worth entertaining. And yet, there would have to have been a reason. The words could not themselves have counted as a form of explanation. There wasn't a device that allowed for such a possibility. If not an explanation, then what? The writing retained its clarity even though answers were held not so much in the distance but without that form of questioning that would actually elicit them.

Writing, however, did not just occur. Of the many prompts that led him, looking was central. Moving between looking and writing had always defined forms of relation. He looked. In looking, he was claimed as much by objects and faces as he was by works of art. In the space of this movement he was continually situated. He found himself. He was held by modes of saying. Avowal then concession. What could and could not be said was constantly defined then redefined by the interplay of place and modes of writing.

From elsewhere something beckoned. It was as though..... And the ensuing stillness could not but allow.....

2) *Looking in Tours*

He started stories, but they were only ever beginnings. They foundered as they began.

Sitting in the breakfast room in an inexpensive hotel in Tours, from the table at which he was having his meal he could see the lift. As it opened it revealed the mirror that comprised its back wall. As the doors opened he could see himself seeing. His reflection was held until they closed.

Thus far the opening stages what is necessary. A space of looking, reflection and containment has been established.

Looking around him at those who like himself seemed either to enjoy or simply need to take breakfast at a surprisingly early hour, early enough to bear traces of the melancholy of the night, he couldn't help but notice a woman who was hastily finishing her coffee. Just as she took the last gulp, she sat back and seemed to draw breath. Were the rush to have been for a train or for an appointment for which she was already late it would have been explicable. There was, however, no indication that she was leaving the hotel. Her hair was still damp and yet to be brushed. The pullover she was wearing would have necessitated a scarf. Her neck was exposed and there was already a cold wind blowing. He continued to look precisely because a momentary glance was no longer possible. He had become curious. She remained oblivious to this curiosity. He watched her walk to the elevator. Now, he was convinced that her rush was without cause. As the doors opened, he noticed himself looking. Her back remained turned towards him. In the mirror he could see her face. She could see his. As she moved some still clumped strands of damp hair away from her face, he saw her smile. Was at him? Was it at the oddity of an encounter with a reflection? Or was the smile indifferent? Not indifferent to her, a smile will always have its reasons, but occurring as though he wasn't there.

He began to separate the possibilities. The prompt to write them down was resisted and yet as they began to take on discreet forms they started to overlap. He could not escape from what now seemed inevitable, namely, that more than one of them could have been at work. As this thought began to register it occasioned in him the need to pause. He could only ever respond, or, as a preliminary gesture understand what confronted him, if he could see in the weave the constitutive elements. He knew that this was why he only ever paused. Not because the weave remained, but because the task was always impossible. There weren't separable threads. The only reality was the weave.

The problem only arises once there is a complex. It emerges not because there are differing possibilities but because those possibilities cannot be separated.

What occurred next was of course of no surprise. He confronted it continually. A confrontation with what continued to impose itself on him. Perhaps, it was a need in disguise. What endured was another possible project. He had to rid himself of the restriction, the haltering and thus distance, what he had described to himself in the past as an insistent pause, within which he worked. The imposition was neither welcome nor unwelcome. That would not have been the point. It defined him. More importantly, it came to define for him a certain relation to events.

Here, the problem arises. It seems both arcane and banal. What is an event? The problem of the weave and the strand, the problem that both occasions and stops the writing, is no more than the problem of an event's quality.

He was suspicious of his capacity for introspection. He had known that while it gave rise to a form of satisfaction the restrictions it imposed had begun to stifle him. What form of connection could there be between his continual halting and clumps of damp hair?

He remembered reading an account of Pearl Harbour. The date was still clear to him as it occurred just a few days before his father's birthday. He often wondered if, at what would have been his father's twenty-second birthday, the conversation would have been dominated by what took place. They would have known that over 2400 American serviceman had been killed, 18 boats were sunk and 357 planes were destroyed. His father was already in the army, already posted to North Africa; nonetheless they would have had a drink to celebrate his birthday. Talk would have moved from pleasantries to a discussion of the impact of that day of destruction. The talk would not have been innocent; no one would have been indifferent to the possibility

of America's entry into the war. By then, two weeks after
the Japanese raid, they would have known that America
was involved in what would become the Second World War.

If some of the strands were clear the complication arose
precisely because Pearl Harbour only emerges as an event
in the days after December 7 1941. Pearl Harbour did not
occur on that day. Its occurrence happened afterwards. If
Pearl Harbour exists as an event, then the question is for
whom? Who would give it that name? Moreover, who would
insist on that name?

*In every act of writing there are differing projects at work and
thus different voices competing for supremacy. There can be no
naïveté here.*

He was still in the breakfast room when she returned, He
has been preoccupied first with the newspaper and then
with trying to catalogue the day's differing projects. In the
end they were one and the same. All centred around writing about Mantegna's ***Christ in the Garden of Olives***. This
was what, after all, had brought him to Tours. What he had
to get to was a type of writing that moved beyond simple
description and which, nonetheless, allowed detail a genuine presence. He has spent years sitting in front of different paintings. If you stay for long enough, he once explained, you can watch them live. If there is an analogy
then it is with a naturalist. The life of a painting, perhaps
even more so of a sculpture, needs to be observed with as
much care and with the endless patience that watching an
animal would demand. Life is an activity. Mere description would equate the painting with an already dissected
corpse. Neither would be adequate to the presentation of
life. What, then, to write?

When the lift door opened, though only for a moment, he was present with her. She was standing while his reflection was next to her. The absurd situation of intimacy without intimacy. Though for whom? As she left, she turned to face him, or at least she turned such that she could have seen him. Indeed, that was it. If there is a space which occasions longing then it is the one opened by the difference between the reality of eyes that meet and eyes whose differing holds never lock or if they do then rather than having been seen there is the look of indifference. The look in which having been seen and not noticed occur simultaneously. All this took place in an instant. There wasn't a flurry of exchanged glances in which there would be looks that oscillated between the furtive and the pleading. There was nothing other than a space in which differing fields of vision intersected, a space without patience. The uneventful. Attempting to fill that space is the project that defined what he took writing to be.

Perhaps that was it. Seeing has to have its own history. Its own implications. Otherwise it is held by the drag of utility.

Mantegna had long exercised a hold. As with any trip to a gallery or museum there were expectations that were in part created by the research he had already done and the now familiar activity of looking at paintings. There was the need to encounter the researched object for the first time whilst remaining open to the possibility that despite whatever competencies he may bring there were going to be elements that would surprise him. The force of any surprise cannot be anticipated. It was about an openness defying any momentary lapse. Nothing could be paused.

What would it mean to see it for the first time? Of course, there would not have been a first time since he had studied many reproductions. He had read in one of the commentaries that had preoccupied him recently that the painting in Tours may not have been by Mantegna working alone. He may only have assisted with its creation. What this opens up is the possibility that a work's relation to a name may be arbitrary. This possibility will preoccupy the scholar. He however was content to note that attribution seemed to be contestable. The genuine is constructed and reconstructed. What interested him far more was that the work had a history of being seen. There must have been many instances in which viewing was productive. There will have been stories, moments of inspiration that accompany and must continue to accompany the work. Were all of them the result of having been surprised? He knew that he could not participate in any unequivocal manner in furthering such a project. What he wanted to know was what they saw.

The clearest instance of Mantegna's work being seen is the drawing Dürer's did in 1521 in which the body of Christ occupies a similar position. If Dürer has not seen the actual painting, Mantegna's was completed in 1495, then he must have seen a drawing of it. What perplexed him was what Dürer had seen in the work. While taking up that question would continue to structure his current writings, there was always another element one that continued to be at work in the openings that had confronted him in the breakfast room that morning. He confronted another task. Though he had already conceded to himself that there are no longer clear moments of differentiation.

Looking for a hint, an answer gestured at, will fail. In the surround, in what is a tightening of concerns, detail is both impossible and necessary.

He remained tentative. Looking at Mantegna's painting he saw within it a type of severance. The work was in fact two paintings that are presented as one. There was a sustained lack of consistency of scale. It could be over-looked because a sense of perspective allowed the eye not to see it. Having looked however it could not be avoided. The figures in the garden could not be equated with painting's other elements. The tree that divided the work allowed the discrepancy momentarily to escape from view. The effect of the severance clear. It enabled the work's narrative to be registered while at the same time giving the figures in the garden a dramatic quality. Moreover, it is a quality that would have been undone were their presence to have been assimilated to the overall narrative of the painting. The work demanded the discrepancy. Was that what Dürer had seen?

He knew that in the evening at dinner, he had opted to take his meal in the hotel, the reasons pertained to practicality, he would be alert to the possibility of her return. There was no sense in which he wished for conversation. What he wanted was something else. He was sure that she would not return to eat. Just by looking you could predict in advance from their demeanour and style those who would return to the hotel in the evening for dinner rather than seek out restaurants. In part it had to do with eating alone. Eating by oneself in the hotel in which you are staying seemed acceptable. The activity almost had a domestic edge. The solitude while announced was nonetheless muted.

What now could he say? Maybe seeing her in the morning and having held open the possibility of having been seen, perhaps looking to be seen, was the event he had been after. Is this what he understood?

3) *Looking at Poussin*

First it was the drawings. The lines seemed to have a quickness to then. As though their position on paper could be equated with speed's visual presence. Each one produced with a controlled rapidity even though the production would only ever be a series of lines. For these sketches there could not have been anything preliminary. They were it. With them work had both began and in most instances ended. This quick succession of lines had results which often struck him with a force that many finished works could never have had. He knew that these drawing and sketches were not incomplete as though all that they demanded was further work. Nor were the simply provisional. The lines were arranged. Again he knew that he was struggling to find the words. It wasn't as though there were terms that simply escaped him. A subtler problem was in play. In part it was related to the question that had long bothered him. In these sketches he could see a different sense of order. Nonetheless, what mattered was order's presence. While he could content himself for a moment with such thoughts— order's necessity etc—questions still endured. What remained had persistence. Words couldn't be simply summoned. Giving them presence was endlessly easy. Rather, the thoughts that preoccupied him slipped past words. The latter only ever being provisionally engaged. Possibilities were touched upon without ever being filled out. Words didn't remain empty. There was a continual elision. However, this movement, the opening occasioned by an engagement that could not be sustained, continued to give rise to the spacing which allowed him to write. These spaces were defined in relation to forms of work which were themselves constructed by a type of freedom. Oddly what had to be maintained, and it will involve actions defined by constraints rather than by a simple openness, were the possibilities that this sense of freedom allowed.

Every time he wrote about artworks he was tormented by a 'perhaps'. The frustration it engendered could not always be given voice. For the most part that voice would need to be muted. Arguments should not be ruined in advance. And yet, the frustration remained. He knew that as he wrote its voice was present. The key was however always different. The 'perhaps' would lighten arguments.

He had just seen Poussin's extraordinary painting of Diogenes having abandoned his cup and drinking henceforth only with his hand. A moment that was integral to the account of Diogenes' life prompted Poussin's work. The painting was completed in 1648. It was a commission. Poussin was earning his living. The principal characters of the painting, Diogenes and his student, occupy only a small part of the work. On one level their visual presence could be construed as a minor event.

While the distant hills continued to draw the eye in—drawn into a form of vanishing—the point of entry brings with it a return. The eye comes back. It returns to the moment at which the space of light's absorption meets the place of light's reflection. The river as the place of return carries shadow and reflects light. Lines are created and held in place. Borders, edges crossing and overflowing are created and positioned by the work of light.

The eye is held by the work. An apparent tranquillity undone. What then of the ostensible subject matter. He was not just perplexed by the work's title—*Diogène jetant son ecuelle*—more generally it was the demand of the title. Was the title an attempt to answer the question of what had been seen? Was it simply a legal requirement that allowed for identification and reidentification? Perhaps the questions that needed to be posed had more to do with the relationship between the eye and the title. What really mattered—at times the insistence of its concerns would have to be lost—was the act of seeing. There was no point succumbing to whatever it was that had been thought problematic in the relationship between the word and the image. Here his concern was with a quality that is different.

The eye sees. The title names. Does the eye see the named?

He would need to return.

4) *Looking at Her*

Looking at her face, and the detail he could still recall, looking at her while she stared at something else that was passing before them. Her looking at it and his looking at her created a space. Within it, what he could see was the site of a future that was already fleeing from him as he watched. What was it about this future that had become, though he knew that it was already that from the start, impossible? Here was a word that had stayed with him. "Impossible". More than that, it was as though the word marked out a specific space of activity, a space in which activity no matter how intense, had no way of opening up. Any future would have already been checked. It was a space in which he felt trapped even though that brought with it, more likely it opened up, within it, its own sense of possibility. Even if there were no way out, it is always possible to pace the space within which the one is held. In there being no way out, no way of moving beyond its already structured sense of continuity, what futural possibility there had been had already vanished. Watching her face meant watching this vanishing. If, within him, there was a now a stilling, an absence linked to impossibility, and then it was inextricably bound up with the vanishing that had pervaded him as he watched her. What gave this moment its fragility was the likelihood that it could have been interrupted. At any moment she could have turned and caught his gaze, holding him with her look. In returning her gaze what possibility there was of allowing flight to have its way—and he knew that he had to add that this flight was the truth of things and that were she to have turned, with their eyes meeting, with his being held in view, then the truth that was the future's vanishing could not have been experienced.

He wondered how this will sound.

The difficulty of its formulation once again began to take its toll on his capacity to describe. The difficulty was linked to a sense of solitude. Perhaps it had created that state. Even now, when solitude had become essential to any sense of continuity he was not sure. He knew that what he had wanted was there to have been someone who could have listened and who could have told him, or at the very least let him know when the words themselves slipped the hold of that measure in which meaning was constrained to lie. He sensed that what he was articulating had meaning. Simple meaning could never have been the issue. What he needed to know was the extent to which the demands of that moment, the moment of fragility, could be described. What had to be acknowledged, though 'how' was the question, was that which had to be held back from interruption in order that it be what it is. The problem lay in his capacity, and he had to admit that if there was going to be failure then it was his. It would have been as though he had misused the very language that he was deploying to present—was that the word?—the issues that had begun to take him over.

And to have taken him over to the extent that the only way in which he could find himself was articulated within the very practices that he had begun to describe.

"Impossibility" was the very name for what traversed his undertaking. Not the vanity that lay there prior to realizing the end that he wanted. Its being the name presented him with a sense of clarity. The precise nature of that clarity was what endured. Providing the setting in which the need to account, perhaps even to explain, if only to himself, what had taken place.

Was impossibility simply negative, or was there, in this apparent difficulty something else that could open up, and in opening up allow for additions that were yet to be adequately discerned. What he had always hoped for, perhaps not so much in the result but in the capacity, was that in giving an account there would be this other quality He knew that in all of this what remained as a necessity—though one again he felt it was a necessity without a voice—was this other element. At a certain point what had begun to emerge was the possibility that somewhere there had been a secret and that part of what resisted, part of what eluded his grasp was its content.

5) *Looking Back*

For whom do we long? For what do we long? These questions and his thoughts began to trail.

What he thought he had lost, or so it seemed, and it defined him then was the capacity for love. While his feelings were often taken, 'his heart won', or that what used to be said—at times he felt himself swept up within feeling whose control was no longer his. In the midst of it all something was lacking. Not an absence, it was as though, and the memory of this moment still held him, a capacity had gone. Personal relations had neither vanished nor died off; what he felt was that he had died within them. Here was a death of sorts. Not a walking death. He carried within himself what had been a vital part, though which had ceased responding. It was simply as though he saw. Looking through the space of feeling, whilst not feeling. However odd this situation may have been, it had by now intruded into his daily life. It was what he wanted to explain. (What he wondered was whether there would be a type of life in the explanation.) More was involved. Something else stayed with him. Staying, it worked in tandem—an odd harmony indeed—with what he would continue to identify as a vanishing capacity. The second, and he knew that its explanation would have to blend with the first, allowed for a pattern to be given. Here he waited. Again he knew that he was fumbling. It was the recurrent difficulty. The one haunting explanation or at least unsettling it, if what he had wanted to do was give an account. He paused, thinking, almost audibly as though fine threads of sound were touching his thoughts, that if he had to explain this other element, it would allow him space. Almost as an attempt to clarify his thoughts he wondered if what he was after was a break in the hold of what he knew was causing him to founder? It would not be a break. After all, it was that hold that allowed him to think, and which was causing him to begin to explain. It remained with him as a debt. This other element had structured relations. And yet, he felt that were there to be an explanation then the recourse to a language of utility would have denied the way this particular fantasy exercised itself. He knew, though this was always going to be the source of difficulty, that certain projections were bound up with questions that he took to be moral. Questions to do with proper actions. Once this was thought, he sensed its absurdity. Nonetheless, the thought was there. He knew that he would have to face the complex series of moments—some of which were reasonable while others had a certain absurdity; nonetheless all were marked by a reality demanding a response. The explanation would depend on it.

She was not there if that meant she was by his side. Nor was she there if that were to have involved discussions and jointly made decisions. Nor moreover was she there, if presence is defined by the possibility of touch. And yet, and here he sensed the growing frustration, was there to be an account of this? Perhaps he had to start with the question that stayed with him and work back. That way, at least, he could connect those things that had begun to deliver him over to the world in ways that allowed him the pretension of no longer being able to recognize himself. Of course, that was absurd. He did recognize himself. There was something else. While recognizing himself—he knew that he was there and that his thoughts, even his actions, were moving in one direction rather than another—he failed to see himself, or at least see himself completely, in what he saw and even at times in what he did. Both were true. It was as though in turning towards a mirror or in catching a glimpse in a window as he walked by there was, at the same moment, seeing and not seeing. Recognizing and not recognizing—both were there, defined by a distance that accounts for this odd division. What marked out these occurrences is that they did not just pertain to vision, as though all that it took was the eye. In fact the opposites was the case. What was really going on had to do with how he saw himself. There would have to be more. The fumbling of his attempts was beginning to exhaust him.

In a way it was simple. She was ever present. They had met a few times and each time had stayed together for only short periods. Afterwards, there had been intermittent letters. He had enjoyed writing them and he knew that while responses were often later in coming than he would have wanted, they were still there. Letters appeared. It was not just that he found the letters to have become more personal, what was happening is that their relationship was growing within them. The question arose because the time between the moments when he took up his pen, and the moment of their meeting, was increasing. He wrote and there were responses. The letters always ended with an intimate turn usually however in another language in order that the intimacy be both announced and then distanced—as if it could only be written whilst being simultaneously withdrawn. The question emerged. To whom was he writing?

Which figure was there in the thoughts that arose once he turned from a letter? Though the turn was always from the letter's tangible presence to its presence as a source of memory and invention. He knew, since this was always going to be the problem, that it was this turn that had to be given centrality. The divide—what he had always referred to as a turn enabled the problem to persist. The relation continued. In describing it—and he knew that this is what he had to do - what he wondered was whether or not it could be excised from its position within the activity of memory that persisted precisely by building and rebuilding what was there. If you worked on a memory, could what had been there initially and which prompted all that was taking place now—be uncovered? He suspected that the question was a foolish one. He knew, no matter how attractive the link between memory and a type of archaeology might be, the absence of any real content within such a link was overwhelming. Despite what he knew to be true, the presence of such truths made little impression on him. Part of what was occurring now was occasioned by the irruption of an emotional state that recognized truths, incorporated them, but remained untouched. Even though he knew that he could never be sure, there was a type of certainty that inhabited the thought that part of his survival depended on remaining in touch. He knew, however, that it would lead to an inevitable demise. Though of what he was not, at least at that stage, sure.

He knew where to start. Or at least he knew the question with which to begin. Could he give an account of the first meeting? An encounter which took place and which continues to exercise its hold. What intrigued him, then as now, was the possibility that a chance meeting could have been one for which there might have been a plan. While the plan would not have been worked out in advance, there were other possibilities. Even then it would not be a plan that would try to incorporate such an encounter within the movement of "things." He knew that he used the term "things" both to announce and then to preclude what he would publicly express as the 'nonsense of fate.' Privately his thoughts varied only slightly though they were tinged with a certain agnosticism. While fate accounted for nothing - it was, of course, to be part of the account of aspects of history whose disturbing presence still exercised its hold. Fate, was a simply a failure in that it accounted for nothing real. Fate was one of those terms that, despite its chequered history carried with it little that was satisfying. Fate was just too easy, or if not to easy then too disturbing. Any evocation of fate plotted no more than the point where astrology intruded into history. He had always baulked at the term. If polemic had been an option his formulation was clear: History wasn't humbug; the talk of fate was however.

If chance had been part of a plan—part of something that separated it from the facile account of things - then there had to be more involved. He was convinced that an allowance had to made for the possibility that while preparation had not been undertaken if such activities were thought to be intentional, there could still have been a type of preparation. And here he stopped. It was though within his more general reflections he had come across an idea that insisted precisely because it was obvious. What was obvious was of course a possibility that, until this moment, he had never entertained. The obvious strikes you. It only ever has that quality after the event. While this had revealed to him something about the nature of the obvious, what it also introduced was the recognition—and he would clearly use this recognition in whatever account he was to give of what had taken place—of a link between mood and what occurred.

There are many openings, or directions that allowed for an understanding of the way things take place.

He smiled since once again he was forced to allow "things" to enter into his explanation. A term that, was allowed entry on the condition that it could never satisfy. (Though this was not a conscious decision.) In being used it had to be qualified. Though, and this was a thought that had occurred many times before, this may be what is necessary. It could just be that such terms are introduced because they mark the place of and the need for an addition. Almost another writing that incorporates their presence but incorporates them only on the understanding that there has to be something else. As though it was a type of explanation whose strength lay in the necessity of its marking a place. As though what came after could not function were its place not prepared—a preparation indicated and sustained by the writing of "things ' but which would not have worked without that mode of entry. Equally, and he had long liked forms of reciprocity, "things" as a term could not stand on its own. It was not that it was a worthless, let alone without meaning. On the contrary its worth lay in what it allowed.

What setting would that need? What type of reflection is demanded in order that this position of "things" take on some sense. Once he would have argued that it was all obvious. When he heard argument for simplicity—almost as though the simple and the straightforward were virtues—he now knows, and knew almost intuitively, that such positions simply failed to understand how things are. It was in this regard that he had often thought about how themes of continuity and discontinuity formed part of one's life. A cough or a pain is harmless precisely because earlier ones were safe. Continuity is safety realized. The need for safety was bound up with continuity, which in turn was bound up with the necessity to distance any possibility of an interruption or a discontinuity. As he thought it through the point became clear. Continuity is the only way of precluding death—or at least not allowing symptoms to become harbingers of death. Death was not simply the most emphatic form that interruption could take, it was announced—or more importantly its possibility was announced—in any moment that was discontinuous with what had come before. While all of this had an unrealistic air to it—after all death happened and there will always be some moments that are discontinuous with others—there was an element that was true. What was clear was that the fear of death was inextricably connected to the way time was felt and lived. The only way to allow for another way, one other than the one provided by continuity and safety, was not to have mastered death but to have incorporated it such that it became part of life. Not death as the inexplicable outside but as another moment within life.

One first seeing her, he recognized neither potential nor its absence. Why use a term such as "potential?" He had to be strict with the terms that he used. Not that he believed that at a certain point he will have gotten it right and the explanation would then unfold almost with a natural logic of sequence. More simply, it was because there were words which, quite simply, when used denied both the feelings at the time, let alone what he really felt now. Now, that it was all in the past, though that "all" was, of course, exactly what his present consisted of. Hence his need to return to a form of questioning and forms of expression that would allow not accuracy—for there could never be accuracy—but at least a type of proximity. What he really disliked about terms such as "potential," when used in this context, is that they bore a load that forced them in a direction away from the possibility that they may actually have. In regard to the word "potential" it was almost ironic. The term carried with that which would deny its very nature.

Having thought about what the French called *l'ennui* - a word, which, now that it figured in English, seemed to resist whatever clarification translation would bring—he remained perplexed. Was it a mood? He had once tried to sketch an essay on boredom. As though writing about it would rid him of its hold. Moods, of course, are not chosen. They cannot be shaken off by a simple change of mind. There was little point saying, "don't be bored" (this was, of course, a truth known by every child, but forgotten by every adult) as though the intended response was that the mood could be shrugged off. What was it then?

He complicated matters.

He knew that without her, a hold had begun to exert itself over him. This being 'without' was not a continual state. Often his thoughts did not even move in her vicinity. His thoughts passed her by: neither touching, nor not touching—simply passing by. The recognition that he was 'without' overcame him. He was overcome by the thought. Without wanting to respond he knew there was little choice. It was as though he was positioned by it. Being positioned was how he would describe it later. Later, when he thought that all this could take the form of a letter. Now, he knew that the letter would be impossible. To whom could he actually address what had gone on? 'Gone on' and yet still going on.

After having been here, having spent those short times together, her departure could be noted in what remained. These were moments of immediacy: touch, smell, the insistence of moments. Then, and by 'then' all he meant was at least initially, her not being there was simple. She was not there. Her touch, he could still feel. Most of all it was a smile. And a look of dazzled happiness in her eyes. He smiled (was even this act a type of recall?); these formulations were easy. And yet, despite that ease they carried a certain truth. It was not the first time that they had been used; he had rehearsed them. But rehearsing, in this sense, only marks the distance from what there had been, and his being without her. If there were a voice, perhaps that would have done. Not her voice, but something voicing what had been.

And the 'without'? Was there going to be a way to deal simply with this question?

Whatever it was that his being without her amounted to, he sensed that it was like a mood. It settled upon him. As though waking in a mist, every moment was blurred. There would be little point in the attempt to move beyond it. All that would happen was that for a time each moment was lived—and for others there could not have been any real difference in his behaviour; he drew some comfort from this—without her. What fascinated him, and this too would form an important part of the letter that would be written, is that this 'without' almost had a positive content. He was without her. He supposed that was how she was present to him. There was some comfort in this. What was he without? On one level the question is almost banal in its stupidity—he often allowed the words 'banal' and 'stupid' to work together in a single formulation, though if he were honest he would have admitted that he thought them interchangeable. The fact that they were not viewed as such allowed him the freedom to compound descriptions by using them one after the other. The problem was that despite the restriction of an apparent banality the question was real. If what remained was simply that memory, and it was that memory that was the subject of reinvention—and now the true meaning, or if not meaning then the drama, of the word rehearsal would have to figure, then what was he really without. After all, she had remained. The questions—what remained? Who was she?—became, for this very reason the more intense. Longing prevailed. Looking.

Notes on Poetry

For Karen MacCormack

*   Waiting to see what poetry would bring involves
forms of expectation. Poetry expects. Equally, it is expected. An expectation therefore that brings poetry into play
without the need for a defining *not*. Poetry cannot be constrained by forms of definition that were preceded by or
which arrive at a *not*. As though what poetry is *not* is a
source of understanding. As though negation, poetry's
own, would have been an opening to poetry. The limit is
clear. Poetry defined by a series of negations cannot open
beyond an insistent *not*. Trapped, unable to traverse an unending set of knots. As a result unable, even, to encounter
itself. Expectations therefore would have been defied. Were
those expectations to have been stilled, poetry forced back
on what it is not, a forcing that is not even poetry's having
been abandoned to *itself*, but its having been abandoned
as such, even then there is a remainder, a feeling still endures. Enduring as a form of awaiting. Hence the question:
Is there another lead, one leading to another *known*? While
what is being asked clears a space, even forms of address
remain elusive.

*   Continuing. Even if negation's hold—poetry defined by a *not*—fails, other avenues while appearing to
be open only ever endure as forms of closure. Were there
to be one then the way ahead would have to break open.
Thus moving beyond the knot/not that seeks to hold poetry. Rather than the apparently countering force of another negation, if there were a way out then it stems from the
enclosing. Even though it may have been enclosed poetry

turns within that enclosure. It turns to *itself*. This *itself* has to be remembered. Remembered, retained and, in the end, affirmed. After all, what truth would there be in a showing that was brought to poetry? Rather than a definition given by that which came from without—from the outside—what if there were another way? The question itself stalls any precipitate onward rush. In that stall there is the intimation of an actual opening. Rather than questions of either form of content predominating, let alone of poetry staging, presencing what it is not, what if it were possible to begin with two simple assertions. They begin with poetry. Beginning with the inescapable. *There is poetry.* To which the following should be added: *What there is sustains a sensibility.* Poetry is the latter's object. A sensibility that touches on what there is. The *there is* of poetry. Perhaps then there would be another touch. What is touched upon would then be poetry's own object.

*   What sustains? What is sustained? Within these questions language is allowed another quality. Allowing language a presence in which poetry's insistence is there in a form of work. However, that work involves relations and thus differing forms of address. Poetry depends upon a type of sensibility. Reading work, allowing for its poetry, responding thereby to what was expected.

*   Poetry's occurrence pertains to a sensibility to the given that is linked to a type of allowing. There is a sensibility which is itself an occasioning, sensible to the given as the occasioning of language and thus to language already being the site of work. If there were a link to truth then it is not a truth that is shown independently of the work of language. On the contrary, it is the truth about that work. Work is already sited. That site, the work, already bears what *there is*. Bares it.

*   *'Perchè scrivi,/ Perchè tu scrivi in lingua ignota e strana,/ Verseggiando d'amor, e com t' osi?'* Daring, of course has to do with what language occasions. It cannot be a mere state of mind. Nor could it be just one language. The poet knows this. Evoked in this question's answer is the name of poetry itself, which here is *Canzone*. The final line completes. Completing however not by evoking a finality that ends but with the reiteration of poetry as itself a condition of possibility: *"Questa è lingua di cui si vanta Amore."* Poetry as language's work stages and allows.

*   What is there, given to be read, yields to a feeling which opens a return to what is there. (Given within a relation to poetry's own history.) And which is there now as the site of reading. Poetry stages the question—a staging asked within the poem as its own individual question. Its individuality—*'The sense to the cloud of the light, Who can tell me?'*—is both just that, and poetry as a mode of questioning.

*   And yet, poetry though always within the poem, retains the structure of the question to the extent that any answer while evincing a necessary fidelity to what was asked, and it is this fidelity that carries the project of any poem, cannot escape the presence of further, though now unknown, answers. This now's repeatability—a sense of repetition staged in relation to the inevitability of the given—is what can be known of the poem. Poetry answers the poem's question—*'Hast thou found any likeness for thy vision?'*—by returning within it, by its being that answer. Always as *itself*, thus returning to the task that is always there. Invention stays with and is stayed by what *there is*.

*   While the *not* would always fail poetry, the move towards the declarative endures. It becomes a

necessity. That move is, of course, accompanied by another. Sensibility changes. There is a continuity of movement, a back and forth. Though any evocation of an either/or would be to yield to an illusion. As though language plays out within the hold of oppositions. As though language allowed for a constraint of the essential, and thus of its being constrained to its having one single determination that would be there in opposition to another.

*   The declarative remains poetic—poetry—to the extent that the enclosure that it, the declarative, may work to enforce the closure, one that will always have its own specific exigency, is allowed to come undone. This allowing cannot be disassociated from a specific exigency, namely the need or obligation to declare. The declarative therefore, language as a form of declaration, precisely because it must suspend the possibility of poetry, a suspension that can only ever be pragmatic, is itself as tenuous as the poetic. Each is bound to the work of language and each demands that sensibility within which a specific determination can be sustained. It is, of course, always sustained after the event. That event is more complex than first appears. It is language as event—thus the event of language. This however is not the end point. Caution, therefore, has itself become necessary. The event of language, and the *itself* of poetry, are always there at work within poetry as the poem. There is a relation. It involves, equally, the giveness of language's use. The latter, here, takes the form of the history of poetry, a history that incorporates the specific.

*   And the relation? What is this relation? Questions that bring their own sense of complexity into play. A complexity linked to a threefold opening. As a beginning, the relation resists an encounter with the essential by allowing poetry a history. *There is* poetry. Then the relation gives rise to a demand. Of the particular *there is* the question of its presence as a poem. Finally, there is the interplay of what *there is* and language as declarative.

*   *Time numbers motion, yet*...It is, of course this *yet* that marks a break. Not a mere break but an opening. Opening to another time. The line continues, *without a crime / ('Gainst old truth) motion numbered out his time.* Cosmic time meets mortal time. Death is now possible. There is an inversion. A necessity now obtains. Were it not for that inversion there could be no real account of either mortality or finitude. The insistence of the severance occurs with the *yet* that joins them. The *yet* allows for one and the other. The *yet*, of course, becomes the poem. Becoming it by its being the work of poetry. Marking it as a poem. The *yet* turns the opening declaration *Time numbers motion*. Not by turning it against itself but by turning it towards another possibility. It still declares - *Time numbers motion* - though once said what possibilities that it might have entailed, and it is an entailment that always follows a declaration, are refused. The interruptive *yet* demands that the declaration come undone. *There is no other life but this - / Yet this life elects the soul / As refugee or citizen.* The opening expectation, its deliberate singularity, is caused to falter. It stalls. The *yet* both calls upon and sustains that other sensibility. As these lines are read, as the force of the *yet* is encountered, the move forward brings with it another demand. Any declarative force that these openings may have had is now, after the *yet*, dispelled. The opening words are repeated, read and thus always there sounding within the continuity of reading; thus, they are there being always reread; therefore, they are there within and as something else. That something other is poetry.

*   Poetry, on its own, can undo the declaration, though it can declare an undoing. Though introduced and repeated the 'I' can become an impossible source, even of its own continuity. Recounting a biography refusing unity while giving the latter that form of presentation in which the continuous 'I' would no longer be there: *quand' era in parte altr' uom da quel ch' i' sono.*

*   What does it mean, now, to continue? Is love's labour to have lost to another, and then, in having lost, what could poetry say? The saying would be the event. *There is written, her fair neck round about: / Noli me tangere, for Caesar's I am, / And wild for to hold, though I seem tame.* She has noted the writing. In writing she notes it. She is neither Christ nor hind. The interdiction, originally, had been spoken. Mary Magdalene heard the words—*noli me tangere.* On hearing she did not touch. Now, however, hearing has become reading. Touching is still forbidden. Another sense and place of sovereignty is in play. The line traces its movement from Christ to Caesar. Read once *'noli me tangere'* is the forbidding of physicality *tout court.* Christ's body must remain untouched. The refusal of touch as the line continues is different. The difference is staged twice. In the first instance it is there in the move from saying to writing. The words - *'noli me tangere'*—inscribed into the poem, becoming it. The force of that move only becomes clear once the words are no longer Christ's. The addition *'for Caesar's I am'* locates the presence of touching and thus of the physical elsewhere. It is not just another, rather it is Caesar. Moreover, that physicality is given greater extension in the last line's juxtaposition of 'wild' and 'tame.' It is, of course, possible to continue. This is the opening that poetry allows. *There is* poetry.

*   A final note? What could be noted at the end? And this would have to be an act without obligation. *Forse.* In answering it will be possible to begin with what has already ended. Two intertwined paths. Firstly, the beginning is the act of reading. An expectation in relation to what *there is* (to what is already there). A sensibility sustaining it. Poetry has to be allowed. Equally poetry's own allowing is maintained in the process. The other path is one in which reading comes to be matched by writing. The writing of poetry is always retrospective in the precise sense that what is written—and it is never poetry but poems, perhaps more accurately a poem, lines having been allowed to stage poetry; *there is* poetry—begins poetry. Each poem, every line begins poetry again. And if this—this retrospective awareness of poetry's presence - were itself a question? Such a question would be clear: How is this beginning a beginning? In other words, if the question then became one bound up with a declaration that *there is* poetry here, then, while there is no one direct answer to such a question what occurs is the moment in which a form of knowledge—the knowing resisting the work of negation—takes hold.

Armidale, Sydney: January 3-9, 2017.

www.ingramcontent.com/pod-product-compliance
Lightning Source LLC
Chambersburg PA
CBHW030223170426
43194CB00007BA/843